Return to Tsugaru

Travels of a Purple Tramp

Osamu Dazai

Translated by James Westerhoven

KODANSHA INTERNATIONAL LTD.
Tokyo and New York

PHOTO CREDITS

Hanada Chiaki: front cover, 10, 18, 19, 20, 21
Courtesy of Tsugaru Shobō: 1, 3, 12, 15, 16, 17
Kimura Katsunori: 8, 9, 13, 14, 23
Courtesy of Sakanakura Yahachi: 11
Satō Takeji: 22
Courtesy of Ono Masafumi: 25

Publication of this translation was assisted by a grant from the Minami Architectural Bureau in Hirosaki and a subsidy from Hirosaki City.

Return to Tsugaru was originally published by Oyama Shoten in 1944 under the title *Tsugaru*.

LCC 84-48694
ISBN 0-87011-841-2
ISBN 4-7700-1341-8 (in Japan)

First edition, 1985
First paperback edition, 1987

This translation is for Seiko

CONTENTS

ACKNOWLEDGMENTS

When someone presumes to translate from a language he does not know very well into one he does not know well enough, the result almost inevitably becomes a community effort. During the years I have struggled with this book, I have become indebted to so many people that it would add considerably to its production costs if I listed them all. To some, however, my obligation is so great that I would do them an injustice if I did not mention their names, however briefly. It goes without saying that the responsibility for the flaws that undoubtedly still cling to this translation is mine only.

I was particularly fortunate in securing the cooperation of Paul Waley, without whose dedication, which far exceeded the call of duty, this translation would never have seen the light of day. Stephen Snyder's additional editorial advice was invaluable.

Stephen Shaw of Kodansha International deserves a special word of thanks for keeping this book alive when everybody else had given it up for hopelessly moribund.

The translation's survival was assured by the energetic efforts of Tazawa Kichirō, Member of the House of Representatives for the Second Electoral District of Aomori Prefecture; by the extreme generosity of Mr. Minami Kyūnoshin; and by a most liberal grant-in-aid from Hirosaki City.

I owe a lasting debt to the Committee to Publish *Tsugaru* in English, whose members gave unstintingly of their time and energy to see this project through to the end. I am especially grateful for the unselfish support of my colleagues Akiha Fumimasa, Hanada Takashi, and Satō Takeji, and to Professor Ono Masafumi of Aomori Chuō Junior College, who, apart from everything else, was an inexhaustible source of information.

Professor Sōma Shōichi of the Jōetsu University of Education kindly shared the fruits of his research and scholarship with me.

Of the many colleagues at Hirosaki University who assisted me in preparing this translation, I must single out Professors Ezure Takashi, Fukumura Tamotsu (now of Chiba University), Osada Sadao (now retired), Osanai Tokio (now retired), Sasaki Kōji, and Torao Toshiya (now of the National Museum of Japanese History). My friend Koide Tsunao, who helped me so much in the initial stages of this translation, unfortunately did not live to see its completion.

If the staffs of the Hirosaki University Library and Hirosaki City Library ever tired of digging up yet another dusty chronicle or long-forgotten scholar, they never showed it. Without their help, my notes and appendices would never have been finished.

Mr. Takahashi Shōichi of Tsugaru Shobō, Mr. Sakanakura Yahachi, and Mr. Hanada Chiaki allowed me to make use of their invaluable collections of old photographs. Reproductions and new photos were provided by the indefatigable Kimura Katsunori.

Though it is customary to thank one's spouse at this point, I have special reason to do so. From the beginning my wife was closely involved with this translation: she answered my endless questions, checked my English against the original, suggested better translations, and until the final stages of revision functioned as the last Court of Appeal. Her modesty forbids me from printing her name as cotranslator. The least I can do is dedicate this book to her.

Editor's Note: With the exception of the author's name on the jacket and title page, Japanese names are given in the Japanese order—family name first.

TRANSLATOR'S PREFACE

The Tsugaru Peninsula, which forms the northeastern tip of the main island of Japan, has always enjoyed the mystique of being slightly different from the rest of the country. Part of its exotic reputation may have been due to the fact that Tsugaru was the last dwelling place of the Ainu on Honshu, but it may perhaps more justly be attributed to the simple factors of distance and unfamiliarity. Tsugaru has always been fairly accessible by sea, but since it lies on the Japan Sea coast, the "backside" of Honshu, there was comparatively little traffic with the shogun's capital at Edo, and overland connections with the rest of the country were primitive. Because most of its area consisted of marshes and swamps, Tsugaru was largely left to itself until its subsequent agricultural development made it economically more interesting to the central government.

Considering this long history of semi-independence and isolation, it is not surprising that the inhabitants of Tsugaru are extremely conscious of their own identity. Although culturally they are very much part of the Tōhoku, or northeastern, area of Honshu, their customs and traditions have over the ages taken on an unmistakable Tsugaru character. They are proud of their speech, a fiendishly difficult variant of the Tōhoku dialect, which even people from the eastern half of the same prefecture understand only with difficulty. The Tsugaru people are reputed to be plain folk—rough and difficult to get along with at first, but honest and simple, if a bit too fond of *sake*. And they have, as they themselves will add, hearts of gold.

Such a character may strike the modern Western reader as rather agreeable, but until recently Tsugaru was generally considered one of the most hopelessly backward regions of Japan, and its people, country bumpkins lacking in most of the redeeming graces of civilization—starting with language and manners, to name just two. One can hardly blame the Tsugaru people if they occasionally portray their country as an Arcadia and Hirosaki, the regional capital, as a bulwark of rural culture, a northern Kyoto.

The truth is less idyllic. Though the soil of the Tsugaru Plain is fertile enough, its winters are long and harsh and its summers short and comparatively cool, so that every year the harvest is a gamble—even nowadays, as the disastrously cold summers of 1980 and 1981 proved. Statistics quoted by Dazai show that the rice crop used to fail once every five years on the average, and since crop failures tended—indeed, still tend—to come in clusters, the people of Tsugaru have suffered through periods of terrible starvation. Like the peasants in other poverty-stricken parts of Japan, they were forced to supplement their diet with "wild vegetables," edible plants that most people would reject as weeds but which provided the nourishment without which they would otherwise have died. Many died anyway. During one eighteenth-century famine, a visitor to Tōhoku reported that women would instinctively close their legs and choke their babies as they were born. Under such circumstances it is understandable that the Tsugaru people turned inward, huddled together in their villages, and looked with suspicion on visitors from beyond the next hamlet.

Such grinding poverty never produces high culture; the most one may expect is a certain level of craftsmanship. Tsugaru produces a fine hard lacquer with a deservedly high reputation, but its attractiveness lies in its finish, not in its design—it is the product of artisans, not of artists. The same goes for other regional crafts, which are still to some extent cottage industries. By and large one may say that the cultural and artistic traditions of central Japan had very little impact on the people of the Tsugaru Plain, who for centuries were happy if they managed to stay alive. So if the people of Tsugaru are different, it is not because of some innate spiritual quality, but because of their geographical isolation and their history of poverty and hardship.

Thanks to better education, improved roads, and the coming of television, what differences once existed are rapidly disappearing. But before the war the peculiar character of the Tsugaru region was conspicuous enough to be recognized elsewhere in Japan, enough at least to warrant a special volume (number seven) in the "New Fudoki Series" of the Oyama Publishing Company—a *fudoki* or gazetteer being an ancient topographical record of one region, with information on its geography, history, customs, and so on. As the author of its volume on Tsugaru the Oyama Company picked Dazai Osamu. Dazai had already written some fifteen volumes of largely confessional fiction, had twice been runner-up for the prestigious Akutagawa Prize, and was well known both for his writings and his bohemian habits. Most importantly, he was a native of Tsugaru.

Dazai badly needed the money, but as we shall see there were other, more personal, reasons why he was only too ready to accept this commission. Oyama approached him in early May 1944. On the twelfth of the same month, Dazai left Ueno Station for Aomori, where he was met by Tonosaki Yūzō ("T."), an old friend from higher elementary school. Dazai pushed on immediately to Kanita, where he stayed for about four days with his friend Nakamura Teijirō ("N."). On one of those days he must have suffered the hospitality of "Mr. S.," Shimoyama Seiji, then administrative head of the Kanita Hospital. Dazai, accompanied by Nakamura, spent one night at Minmaya and another at Tappi (where their signatures may still be seen at the Okuya Inn) before returning to Kanita. After a brief stay in Kanita he moved on to his native home in Kanagi, which he reached about May 22. Some four days later he set out on the second leg of his tour. After a brief stopover in Kizukuri, where he met Matsuki Hidesuke ("Mr. M."), a grandson of his father's elder brother Kanzaburō, he arrived in Fukaura and spent the night there. He then returned the way he had come, spent one night at his aunt's in Goshogawara, and the next day left on what was for him the most important part of his journey, the search for his old nanny Take, whom he had not seen in some thirty years. The book quite properly closes with the emotional reunion of these two, but this was not quite the end of the trip for Dazai. Instead of going straight back to Tokyo, he paid another visit to the Nakamuras in Kanita, and then took a steamer to Aomori. On June 5 he was back in Tokyo. He began to write immediately and finished the final draft the following month. *Tsugaru* was published four months later, in November 1944.

The first readers of this book must have been surprised. Instead of a gazetteer with precise, concrete descriptions of places and customs of interest, they found they had bought a record of Dazai's opinions on himself, love, art, landscape, the writings of Shiga Naoya, and the poetry of Bashō—to mention only a few of the digressions. Almost as a sop to those readers who are genuinely interested in Tsugaru, he throws in some quotations from encyclopedias and popular reference books, with a few perfunctory and very much by-the-way accounts of things he saw from his train window—not nearly enough to fulfill the purpose for which this book was commissioned. When Dazai is able to stay with friends and relatives, he seldom moves far away from the lunch box or the *sake* bottle, and when he is off on his own—as when he travels to Fukaura—he is so bored with his own company that he cannot retrace his steps too quickly. But if he had done what he was paid for and filled the book with more facts and less of himself, we may be certain that *Tsugaru* would now be gathering dust on the shelves, together with its long-since-forgotten companion volumes in the "New Fudoki Series."

We must thank the great novelist Ibuse Masuji (b. 1898) that it is not. Because Dazai had never written straight reportage before, he was at a loss when he accepted the commission. He consulted Ibuse, who had been his literary mentor since his writing debut in 1933. The older writer is said to have told Dazai, "If I were in your place, I would avoid objective descriptions and write the book as a subjective monologue." Dazai obviously took this advice, and so it is that *Tsugaru* is still read as an entertaining and at times deeply moving work of literature.

One occasionally hears claims that *Tsugaru* is, in fact, Dazai's best work, because it is more optimistic, and therefore closer to the "real Dazai," than the despairing masterpieces for which he is best known in Western countries—*The Setting Sun* and *No Longer Human*. But such claims are exaggerated at best. *Tsugaru* is a different sort of work than the novels. It contains several powerfully written passages, but since the book was supposed to be a gazetteer it also contains sections of little literary value. Not that this unevenness should deter the reader—the book amply rewards one's patience. As for "the real Dazai," the great novels of his last years reflect the gloom that had overtaken his personal life quite as accurately as *Tsugaru* expresses the relative happiness that characterized the first years of his marriage. But the existence of these claims, excessive though they obviously are, does indicate that this peculiar work needs to be taken seriously, especially because closer study will reveal that, for all its supposed lightness of tone, *Tsugaru* is a darker book than it seems.

Dazai Osamu was born on July 19, 1909, in Kanagi, near the center of the Tsugaru Plain. He was the sixth son and tenth child of Tsushima Gen'emon and his wife Tane, and received the name

Shūji. The Tsushima family had worked its way up from fairly obscure origins in the eighteenth century to become wealthy land-owners and politicians. Because they sold oil and bean curd, they were less affected than others by the series of famines that hit the Tsugaru region at the beginning and again in the middle of the nineteenth century and were in a position to lend money to the stricken farmers, accepting—which under the circumstances usually meant keeping—the farmers' land as security. By the end of the century, the head of the family was one of the most powerful men in Tsugaru, with enough assets, for instance, to help found a bank. The size of his holdings entitled Dazai's father to run for election in the Lower House, where he served one term, and to a seat in the House of Peers, to which he was elected one year before his death. Despite Dazai's repeated protestations that his ancestors were farmers and he himself no more than a peasant, his origins were decidedly upper-middle-class, which in a poor region like Tsugaru meant virtually the same as aristocratic.

This affluent background does not mean, however, that Dazai enjoyed a happy childhood. He seems to have been a fairly lonely child in a vast household of over thirty persons, among whom he occupied only a very minor position. And even of that position he was not quite certain. Because his own mother was sickly and worn out with child-bearing, Dazai was brought up by his aunt Kie, in whose room he slept and whose four daughters he took for his sisters. His nanny Take, who joined the family in April 1912 as Kie's personal servant, has said that she had always assumed that Shūji was her mistress's child and thus had taken such special care of him. This lends credence to Dazai's later claim that he did not find out who his real mother was until he was seven or eight years old. Uncertainty about his origins was one of the reasons Dazai so readily accepted Oyama's commission.

Dazai's relatives figure prominently in *Tsugaru*, so a simplified family tree may be of use to the reader. Only the names of Dazai's immediate ancestors and of relatives who are mentioned in the book are given:

Tsushima Sōgorō (1833–89) x Tsushima Ishi (1857–1946)
|
Tane (1873–1942)   Kie (1879–1952)
x
Tsushima Gen'emon (born Matsuki Eizaburō, 1871–1923)
|
Bunji   Eiji   Keiji   Shūji   Reiji
(1898–1973) (1901–70)   (1903–30)   (1909–48)   (1912–29)
x   x
Okazaki Rei   Ishihara Michiko
| |
Yō (b. 1925)   Sonoko (b. 1941)
x
Tazawa Kichirō (b. 1918)

It is a little-known fact that for dynastic reasons Dazai's grandmother Ishi was married to her own father's half-brother. This may explain a certain physical frailness that characterized both Dazai's mother and some of his brothers and sisters.

The history of the Tsushima family in the first half of this century is very much the tale of two brothers, Bunji and Shūji. When Gen'emon died on March 4, 1923, Bunji, the eldest son, succeeded as head of the family and as his father's political heir. In 1925, when he was only twenty-seven, he had himself elected mayor of Kanagi, and then went on from strength to strength, serving in various important local functions and in the Aomori Prefectural Assembly until the outbreak of the war. When the Tsushima, like other big landowners, lost their estates in the reforms during the Occupation, Bunji recouped his family's losses by running for prefectural governor, in which capacity he served from 1947 to 1956. From 1958 to 1963, he sat in the House of Representatives, and from 1965 until his death, in the House of Councillors. The family tradition is continued by Tazawa Kichirō, the anonymous son-in-law of Chapter Four, who most recently served as Minister of Agriculture from 1980 to 1982.

Shūji, the fourth surviving son, appears never to have felt at home in Yamagen, the Tsushima family home, and even at elementary school distinguished himself as much for his mischievousness as for his literary talent. Shūji's feelings for his eldest brother seem to have been a mixture of respect and resentment, although he had little reason for the latter, since by all accounts Bunji treated him with understanding and patience. It may partly have been the not uncommon rivalry between two strong-minded brothers, but it probably went deeper than that, for Shūji did cause his family a great deal of trouble.

Even while at Hirosaki Higher School—the predecessor of Hirosaki University—he was marginally involved in left-wing activities and, less marginally, with women. The situation did not improve when in 1930 he left for Tokyo to study French literature at the Imperial University. In October of the same year, Oyama Hatsuyo, a geisha he had met while still in Hirosaki, moved in with him, and he announced his intention to marry her. Bunji obligingly traveled down to Tokyo and offered to pay off the redemption fee Hatsuyo owed the geisha house. Engagement presents were exchanged, but marriage plans foundered on the opposition of the grandmother, Ishi, who despite her advanced age ruled the Kanagi household with a strict hand. She was totally opposed to the idea of her grandson allying himself with a geisha. Shūji found himself struck from the family register and set up as the head of a branch house—a step that formally absolved the family from responsibility to support him. Perhaps in retaliation, perhaps out of shock, Shūji concluded a suicide pact with a girl he had picked up on a drinking spree. The girl drowned, but Shūji survived, and Bunji had to return to Tokyo to hush the matter up.

Things went from bad to worse. Against the wishes of the family, Hatsuyo moved back in with Shūji, who was steadily becoming more deeply involved in the activities of the Communist Party and ultimately had to call on Bunji again to extricate him from its clutches. He postponed his graduation until the last moment, and then failed to graduate altogether—not surprisingly, considering he had hardly ever attended classes. In 1935 he attempted suicide again, and shortly thereafter developed peritonitis, which left him addicted to the painkillers he had been given. It took nearly a year before friends—at Bunji's behest—managed to persuade him to take a cure. While Shūji was in the hospital trying to conquer his addiction, Hatsuyo had an affair with one of his friends. In 1937, Hatsuyo and Shūji, who had won his battle against drugs, unsuccessfully attempted suicide and finally parted for good.

During all these turbulent years, Bunji continued sending his scapegrace of a younger brother his monthly allowance through the good offices of Nakabata Keikichi, an old friend of the Tsushima family, who makes an appearance in Chapter Five. About the only positive thing that can be said about Shūji's activities during this period is that he slowly made a name for himself as a writer of introspective, often fantastic stories in the mode of Akutagawa, whom he had always admired. With some justification, therefore, he was nominated twice for the Akutagawa Prize, and he protested publicly when on both occasions he failed to receive the award.

After his separation from Hatsuyo, Dazai (the pen name Shūji had adopted) drifted, drinking much and writing little. Then things began to look up. He was now twenty-nine years old, and not unnaturally his mother and brothers, who continued to worry about him, decided it was time for him to get married. Unwilling to be actively involved in the negotiations that accompany an arranged marriage in Japan, they sent Nakabata and Kita Yoshishirō, another friend of the family, to Ibuse Masuji for help. Ibuse introduced Dazai to Ishihara Michiko, of Kōfu, Yamanashi Prefecture. Dazai had a reputation to live down, but he managed to persuade the hesitating girl and her relatives of the seriousness of his intentions, and on January 9, 1939, the two were married. The wedding dinner was given at Ibuse's house in Tokyo, Nakabata and Kita representing the Tsushima family.

It seems that Dazai sincerely intended his marriage to be the beginning of a new life. He dedicated himself to his work, writing much and traveling widely to give lectures and collect material for his stories. Now that he had settled down, it was also a good time for reconciliation with his relatives. Bunji's pride was something of an obstacle, but in August 1941, one month after the birth of his daughter Sonoko, Dazai profited from his brother's absence and paid a short visit to Kanagi, his first since 1930. Because his relations with his family were still formally severed, he stayed at Yamagen for only a few hours, but he was greeted warmly by all his relatives, except for the absent Bunji. His mother accompanied him to Goshogawara, where they spent the night at his aunt's, and the next day Dazai returned to Tokyo.

In October 1942 his mother fell seriously ill, and Dazai traveled to Kanagi again, accompanied by his wife and daughter. This time Bunji consented to meet him, and although the reunion was far from cordial, it was tacitly understood that bygones were to be bygones. Dazai and his family stayed for about a week, but the following December Tane's condition became critical and Dazai had to hurry back to Kanagi, which he reached just in time to be at his mother's side when she died on December 10. Some two weeks later he returned to Tokyo, but in January he was back in Kanagi again, with his wife and child, to attend the memorial service on the thirty-fifth day after his mother's death. The visit that Dazai records in *Tsugaru* was therefore the fifth he paid in four years, although it was indeed the first one on which he was able to explore the Tsugaru countryside.

After 1943, Dazai's world slowly began to disintegrate. There are a number of factors that contributed to this general decline in his fortunes, though it is hard to say which was the decisive one. As the war continued, magazines and journals, even newspapers, were forced to close down, thus depriving professional writers like Dazai of an important source of income. More seriously, Dazai was—with some justice—suspected of not fully supporting the war effort, and he began to have problems with the censor. As if this were not enough, he complicated his life further by starting a relationship with another woman, Ōta Shizuko, whose diary was to be a source of inspiration for *The Setting Sun*.

For a while Dazai remained in control of his fate. He managed to survive the war, although at the very end he was forced to evacuate his family on a grueling journey from Tokyo via Kōfu to Kanagi, where from August 1945 to November 1946 he lived in a cottage that belonged to his brother. But after his return to Tokyo, things went quickly downhill, though ironically he was now at the peak of his artistic powers. Especially after the publication of *The Setting Sun* in 1947, he was widely recognized as perhaps the most important voice in postwar Japanese letters. Consequently, he was much in demand as a writer and a speaker, and he pushed himself hard. He was again drinking much more than was good for him, and he resumed his relationship with Ōta Shizuko, who bore him a daughter in 1947. In the meantime, however, Dazai had started yet another affair, with a young widow called Yamazaki Tomie. The combination of hard work and personal problems took its toll. He suffered from insomnia and began to cough up blood, a sign that an old lung problem was acting up again. Writing at a furious pace, he finished *No Longer Human* in May 1948 and immediately started another novel. The strain must have been too much. On June 13, 1948, Dazai and Tomie drowned themselves in the Tamagawa Canal, not far from his house in Mitaka. In a few more weeks he would have been forty years old.

If this survey of Dazai's career has emphasized his personal problems at the expense of his artistic achievements, it is because the facts surrounding the composition of *Tsugaru* may provide a clue to the origin of these problems—not so much by what the book says, as by what it tries to hide.

Ostensibly, Dazai wrote *Tsugaru* as the journal of a quest for love, which in his terminology would seem to mean a willingness to accept others without requiring them to present themselves as different from what they really are. "Pretentiousness" and "affectation" are words that recur time and again in Dazai's works. One of his constant gripes against the world was that it refused to accept him as he was, and his life appears to have been a constant struggle to seem natural—with the ironic result that his naturalness was often forced, and therefore unnatural. "You shouldn't be so damned stuck-up!"—the parting shot of the visitor in his story "The Courtesy Call" (1946)—could serve as a motto for most of his work. One could make a strong case that Dazai's clowning and his debunking of the "refined artist" was an overreaction to this fear of appearing affected.

Tsugaru is studded with suggestions that the shedding of all affectation is a prerequisite for being accepted and loved. Dazai travels incognito, not as the well-known writer, but as the runt of the Tsushima family; his hysteric fulminations against "aristocratic" artists are forgiven him as soon as he confesses to the company on Kanran Hill what is really bothering him; and Mr. S.'s clumsily extravagant hospitality is held up as a shining example of genuine affection. But when Dazai visits Yamagen, his native home, he—like the other members of the household—watches his manners whenever his eldest brother is around. The conclusion he wishes the reader to draw is unstated, but obvious.

The peculiar flatness of Chapter Four may be explained not only from a possible wish on Dazai's part to show up his brother as an affected character or from simple biographical realities, but also from the demands of the book's dramatic structure. For if the narrator's quest for love is the plot, *Tsugaru* actually becomes a typical comedy. The first three chapters are generally upbeat, despite some minor complications; then a downturn in Chapter Four, followed by a low point with the solitary visit to Fukaura; and finally a rapid movement toward a happy ending that almost eludes the narrator—the reunion of Dazai and his nanny Take in Kodomari, when all pretenses are dropped and the narrator experiences peace for the first time in years.

This is no doubt how Dazai wished *Tsugaru* to be read, and it is certainly the most aesthetically satisfying interpretation of the book. It gives an almost cathartic effect to the narrator's search for Take and to Take's emotional outpouring in the concluding pages. Unfortunately that final passage, which is as it were the key to the appreciation of *Tsugaru* and has deservedly become a *locus classicus* in Dazai's work, is ninety percent fiction. Unfortunately, that is, for those who assume that Dazai's account of his wanderings is completely true. Artistically speaking, Dazai made a wise decision when he sacrificed the truth for the sake of dramatic effect, but the real story of Dazai's meeting with Take is just as interesting as its substitute, though for different reasons.

Chapter Five recounts how the narrator arrives in Kodomari. He is quickly directed to the athletic meet where Take has gone with her children, but he fails to find her in the crowd and returns to the bus station, resigned to never seeing her again. When he passes Take's house one last time, he notices that the door is open and he meets Take's daughter, who leads him to her mother. The narrator and Take are both speechless at their reunion and sit down silently to watch the races, but their silence is filled with emotion. At last the two take a walk to the shrine of the Dragon

God, and on the way Take confesses in a "flood" of words how much she has missed Shūji.

Several years ago, Take gave her side of the story in an interview with the scholar Sōma Shōichi. When her daughter Setsuko led Dazai to her booth at the meet, they were accompanied by the chief priest of the temple, an old classmate of his brother Reiji, who had recognized Dazai as he was wandering about the field. Instead of sitting down in peace next to his foster-mother, Dazai drank *sake* with the priest and ignored Take altogether. Not that Take minded. She had almost forgotten Shūji from Yamagen and for the life of her could not see why he had come to visit her. And anyway, she wanted to know how her son did in the races, so she was glad the priest was there to keep Dazai entertained. While Dazai and the priest were raking up old memories, Take decided to go to the shrine of the Dragon God with some of her neighbors. Dazai suddenly announced that he would go along too and said goodbye to the priest, but he had no chance to talk to Take alone. He merely trudged behind the group of a dozen or so middle-aged women and did not speak with anyone.

It was not until that night, which he spent at Take's house, that he had a chance to talk to his old nanny alone, and then it became clear why he had made this trip to out-of-the-way Kodomari. He asked Take: "Am I really Bunji's brother? Am I not Gatcha's [Kie's] child?" And Take told him: "It's true that Gatcha brought you up, but the mother who bore you was Ogasa [Tane], and you are a full brother of Bunji's."[1]

Dazai was almost thirty-five at the time, but all his life he must have worried about the circumstances of his birth. One can only guess at the uncertainty this must have caused him, and at the extent to which it may have influenced—and ruined—his relationship with his brothers and sisters. It may indeed have been one of the principal reasons for the self-destructive behavior he displayed in his twenties.

Dazai's portrayal of Bunji as a stern, cold killjoy becomes more understandable when one realizes the extent of his ambivalence toward his eldest brother. But it is also less credible. If the last, most celebrated pages of *Tsugaru* are fiction, what guarantee do we have that other pages are closer to the truth? The credibility of Dazai's autobiographical writings (though not their quality) becomes generally questionable.

This ambivalance to elder brothers also helps shed light on several other seemingly random bits of information Dazai includes: Yoshitsune, whose name is mentioned frequently in Chapter Three, was killed at the order of his elder brother Yoritomo. In the historical section that opens Chapter Four, Dazai dwells a little longer than necessary on the question of whether the founder of the Tsugaru domain was not actually a younger scion of the great Nanbu clan who had rebelled against his family's overlordship. And an incidental remark about the merits of the painter Ayatari, also in Chapter Four, may after all not have been so very incidental.

Takebe Ayatari (1719–74) is better known as a painter under the name Kan'yōsai. However, he was not only a painter, but a man of letters—a poet who occasionally wrote fiction. He was born in Hirosaki, the younger son of a high-ranking retainer of the Tsugaru clan who died when Ayatari was eleven years old. Some seven or eight years later, while his eldest brother and guardian was away in Edo, Ayatari had a love affair with his sister-in-law, from which at one point they tried to disentangle themselves by swallowing poison. The brother returned to Hirosaki, and Ayatari was forced to leave Tsugaru, never to come back. He was twenty years old at the time of his exile.

Dazai never had an affair with his sister-in-law, but for the rest there is such a close similarity between his career and Ayatari's—

their age when their fathers died and when they left Tsugaru, their abortive suicide pacts, and even their common interest in painting—that one cannot help wondering if Dazai put Ayatari in merely because he happened to be a painter from Tsugaru. Ayatari in fact developed all his artistic talents after he left Hirosaki, which makes Dazai's claims for him as a Tsugaru artist a bit tenuous. But whatever Dazai's motives may have been, it is certainly significant that Bunji's reaction to the name Ayatari is so indifferent. Even if we ignore the possibility that this is an implied rejection of his younger brother, Bunji is still guilty of indifference to the arts and traditions of Tsugaru. In Chapter Four, Dazai appears less interested in showing the powers of love and affection than in getting in a few sly digs at his brother.

On the basis of all this evidence, to which should be added the fact that Dazai himself always referred to *Tsugaru* as a novel, the proper approach to this book is to read it not as a travelogue, but indeed as a work of fiction, whose principal characters—not to be confused with actual persons of the same name—just happen to be called "Tsushima Shūji," "Koshino Take," etc. Lest this sound disingenuous, it is worth pointing out that no less an author than George Orwell, that staunch upholder of the truth, seemed not averse to similar practices in fiction: his "autobiographical" essay "Such, Such Were the Joys" for many years could not be published in Great Britain because of the demonstrably libelous nature of its contents. And how many fans can be found willing to stake their money on the literal truth of Henry Miller's writings? Autobiographical fiction is not exactly an unknown phenomenon in Western letters either.

In the final analysis, Dazai was not interested in writing about his travels. He was writing a book about love. Even the location was not essential. Dazai really met very few total strangers in Tsugaru, and those he met treated him as they would any customer. Yet he wishes the reader to believe that Tsugaru is special because its people are all full of the milk of human kindness. He may be right, but this does not weaken the impression that he had loaded the dice and discovered what he knew he was going to find—or what he wanted to find. For all its factual information, Dazai's portrait of Tsugaru and its people is romantic rather than realistic.

Yet one should not dismiss *Tsugaru* for this reason. Like its great predecessor, Bashō's *Narrow Road to a Far Land*, it is the record both of a journey to an actual place and of a journey to the inner recesses of the author's heart. The things Dazai thought he discovered in Tsugaru, and therefore in himself, were tremendously important to him. In "Fifteen Years," a long, rambling essay he published in 1946, he makes this clear:

> What I discovered during this trip was the awkwardness of Tsugaru. Its clumsiness. Its gawkiness. Its ineptness at cultural expression. Things I have felt in myself. But at the same time I felt a wholesomeness. Who knows but Tsugaru may give birth to a totally new culture. . . . Who knows but it may give birth to totally new ways of expressing love. I returned to Tokyo with a feeling resembling self-confidence because of the pure Tsugaru character of the blood in my veins. In other words, the discovery that Tsugaru did not have what is known as "culture," and that I, as a Tsugaru man, therefore was not in the least a "cultured person," took a load off my mind. And I have the feeling that the stories I wrote after this discovery are a little different because of it.

It would take a special study to decide whether Dazai was justified in that feeling, but Donald Keene appears to think that he had a point. Of the works Dazai goes on to mention, Keene refers to *Otogizōshi* (*Bedtime Stories*, 1945) as possibly "Dazai's most perfect creation, . . . one of the masterpieces of Dazai's art," and also singles out Dazai's retelling of Ihara Saikaku's *Tales from the Provinces* (*Shinshaku shokokubanashi*, 1945). These works, he says, "appeared like shining stars over the sunken horizon of [Japan's wartime] literature." Such praise, coming from such a source, is intriguing, but unfortunately neither of these works has been translated.

But if the dropping of pretensions and the honest if awkward expression of one's feelings is what Dazai learned in Tsugaru, it is not difficult to see how important Dazai's journey to a far land was for the moving creation of Kazuko, the heroine of *The Setting Sun*, and one of the few characters in Dazai's canon with a truly enduring vitality.

Toward the end of "Fifteen Years," Dazai wrote:

> I may be no more than a stupid Tsugaru peasant without any sense of "culture." I know that if you saw me walking through the snow in my galoshes, you would immediately recognize me for the countryman I am. But from now on I intend to cultivate the countryman's bungling ways, his clumsiness, his dimwittedness, his artlessness. If there is anything in my present self that I can build on, it is the Tsugaru peasant.

Unfortunately, the Tsugaru peasant proved to be no match for Dazai's demons.

---

1 (p. xxiv) To understand the ease with which Japanese family relationships may be obscured, one should know that in the Tsugaru dialect *ogasa* and *gatcha* both mean "mother"; the former is a more formal form of address, the latter more familiar. Combine this with the common Japanese practice of addressing people by the name that indicates their position in a family (Mother, Elder Brother, etc.), and one can see why a child may be confused about his exact relationship to the people around him.

Return to Tsugaru

The Snows of Tsugaru

Watery snow and powdery snow,
Grainy snow and downy snow,
Crusty snow and lumpy snow,
    Icy snow.

(From the *Tōō Almanac*)

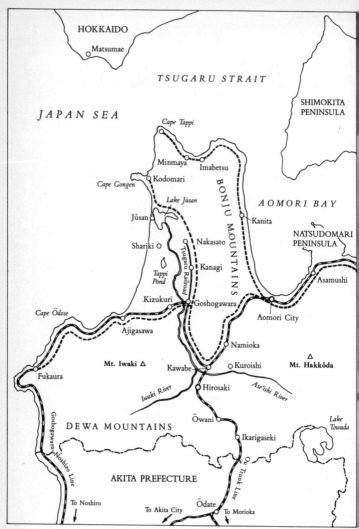

-------- **Dazai's Route**

Introduction

One spring I traveled, for the first time in my life, around the Tsugaru Peninsula in the far north of Honshu. This trip, which lasted for about three weeks, was one of the most important events of my thirty-odd years. Though I was born and brought up in Tsugaru and lived there for twenty years, the only places I knew were Kanagi, Goshogawara, Aomori, Hirosaki, Asamushi, and Ōwani. Of other towns and villages I knew not the least bit.

I was born in Kanagi, which lies roughly in the center of the Tsugaru Plain and has a population of about five or six thousand. Though there is nothing very special about it, in some respects Kanagi affects the air of a larger town. If you were to be generous, you might say it has the freshness of water, and if nasty, you might compare it to a fop of the most frivolous sort.

Some twelve kilometers south along the Iwaki River lies the town of Goshogawara, the collection and distribution center for the products of the region. It has more than ten thousand inhabitants. With the exception of Aomori and Hirosaki there are no other towns with a population of over ten thousand in the region. Goshogawara could be called lively—or noisy—depending on how you look at it. It does not have the feel of a rural town, but is tinged with that frightful loneliness characteristic of big cities, which has already stealthily pervaded small towns like this. The comparison is somewhat inexact, but translated into Tokyo terms Kanagi would be Koishikawa, and Goshogawara, Asakusa.

Goshogawara is where my aunt lives, and when I was a child, I would go to visit her quite often, because I loved this aunt more than my own mother. But I can safely say that until I entered middle school the only Tsugaru towns I knew anything about were Kanagi and Goshogawara. When I sat for the Aomori Middle School entrance examination, the trip seemed a tremendous journey, although I suppose it couldn't have taken more than three or four hours. I recorded the excitement of the occasion in a slightly embellished story that does not accord entirely with the facts and is full of pathetic tomfoolery, but, I believe, nonetheless reflects with reasonable accuracy what I felt at the time.[1]

No one was aware of these sorry little tricks, at which every year he became more proficient. At last he graduated from the village elementary school, and a jolting wagon took him to the train for the small prefectural capital forty kilometers away, where he was to sit for the middle-school entrance examination. The boy's clothes were touchingly bizarre. White flannel shirts having taken his fancy, he of course wore one of those. To the shirt he had attached a big collar in the shape of a butterfly, which he had pulled out from under his kimono collar in the same way you pull out the collar of an open-necked summer shirt over the collar of a jacket. It looked a little like a bib. He had gone to these pathetic lengths in the firm belief that they would make him look a true scion of the aristocracy. He also wore a short formal kimono skirt of a splashed blue pattern with whitish stripes, long socks, and a pair of sparkling black shoes with laces. And over it all, a cloak.

As his father had already died and his mother was sickly, the boy depended for all his affairs on the loving attention of his sister-in-law. Shrewdly taking advantage of her fondness for him, he had talked her into making such a big col-

2

lar, and when she laughed at the idea, he had become really angry, stung to the point of tears at the thought that no one seemed to appreciate his ideas about beauty. Elegance, refinement—not just his aesthetics, but his purpose for living, his whole aim in life, was limited to these notions.

He believed that the elegant way to wear a cloak was to leave it unbuttoned, so that it flapped about dangerously and looked as if it might slip off his puny shoulders at any moment. Had he learned this somewhere, or had he developed this instinct for flamboyance all by himself, without any model?

Since this was just about the first time he had ever visited a city worthy of the name, the boy had on the most elaborate costume he had ever worn. He was so excited that as soon as he entered the little city at the northern tip of Honshu even his way of speaking underwent a complete change. He used the Tokyo dialect, which he had picked up not long before from boys' magazines, but on hearing the way the maids spoke in the inn where he had installed himself, he was not a little disappointed to find that they were using exactly the same Tsugaru dialect people spoke in his hometown, which was, after all, less than forty kilometers away.

This little city on the coast was Aomori. About 320 years ago, in 1624, it was decided that Aomori should be the site of Tsugaru's main port. Construction work began that same year under the direction of the commissioner for Sotogahama. It is said that there were already a thousand families living there at that time. Shipping links were established with Ōmi, Echizen, Echigo, Kaga, Noto, Wakasa, and other provinces. Gradually Aomori began to thrive, and it soon became the most prosperous port in Sotogahama. In 1871, when the feudal domains were abolished, it was made the capital of the newly established Aomori Prefecture.

It stands guard at Honshu's northern gate and is the terminal for the railroad ferry to Hakodate in Hokkaido. But I suppose everyone knows these things. Though it now has more than twenty thousand houses, with a population of over a hundred thousand in all, it does not seem to make much of an impression on strangers. Even allowing for the fact that Aomori could do nothing about the conflagrations that have disfigured its buildings, it is nevertheless hard to figure out exactly where the heart of the city lies.

Confronted with silent rows of strangely sooty, expressionless houses, the traveler feels ill at ease and leaves this inhospitable city in a hurry; but I lived here for four years—years that were extremely important for my future. I recorded my experiences of those days fairly accurately in an early work of mine, "Memories":

> My grades were not very high, but that spring I passed the middle-school entrance exam. I put on a new formal kimono skirt and black socks with my laced boots and discarded my old blanket for a woolen cloak that I slung over my shoulders in a dashing manner—open at the front, buttons undone. Thus clad, I set out for the little city by the sea. I took lodgings at a draper's shop that had a tattered old curtain hung over the entrance; it belonged to a distant relative, to whose care it had been decided I was to be entrusted all those years.
>
> I am the sort of person who is easily excited by the least thing. As a newly registered student I wore the school cap with my kimono skirt even to the public baths, and when I saw myself dressed up like that in the shop windows, I would smile and make little bows at my reflection.
>
> Nevertheless, school was not at all interesting. The building stood on the outskirts of town. It was painted white, and immediately behind it lay the level ground of a park that bordered on the Tsugaru Straits. During classes I could hear

4

the sound of the waves and the rustling of the pines. The corridors were wide and the classroom ceilings high, and all in all I had a good impression of the place, except that the teachers seemed to have it in for me.

From the very day of the entrance ceremony, a physical education teacher used to beat me regularly. He said I was impertinent. I resented this all the more because it was he who had questioned me during the oral part of the entrance examination and had said understandingly that it must have been very difficult for me to study so soon after my father's death, and it was before him that I had hung my head in confusion. Later several other teachers also beat me. I was smirking, or I was yawning—I was punished for all sorts of reasons. I was told my great yawns during class were famous in the teachers' room. I had to laugh at the idea of a teachers' room where they discussed such inanities.

Another boy from my hometown called me behind the sand dune in the school garden one day and warned me: "You really do appear cocky, you know. If you go on getting walloped like that, you'll certainly fail your exams." I was shocked. That day, after class, I hurried home by myself, along the shore. The waves licked at the soles of my shoes, and I sighed deeply as I walked. I wiped the sweat off my forehead with the sleeve of my jacket and saw a huge gray sail lurching by right in front of my eyes.

This middle school still stands on the same spot in the eastern suburbs of Aomori. The level ground belongs to Gappo Park, which borders so closely on the school that it gives the impression of being the school's backyard. Except during the snowstorms of winter, I would pass through this park and walk along the shore on my way to and from school. It was a back street, so to speak, and not too many students took it. But to me it seemed to have an invigorating quality; it was especially attractive on early summer mornings. The name of the family that runs the draper's shop in Teramachi where I boarded is Toyoda, an old and established Aomori store that has been in the hands of the same family for almost twenty generations. The head of the family, who died a few years ago, used to treat me better than his own children, something I will never be able to forget. The two or three times I visited Aomori during the past three years I always paid my respects at his grave and invariably enjoyed the Toyoda family's hospitality for the night.

On my way to school one morning in the spring of my third year, I stopped and leaned against the balustrade of a vermilion-painted bridge and daydreamed for a while. Under the bridge flowed the placid waters of a river as broad as the Sumida. Never before had I been so utterly lost to the world. I always felt people were watching me and so kept up a front at all times. The least thing I did would garner little comments: "He stared at his hands in perplexity," or, "He scratched himself behind the ear and muttered something." So to me a spontaneous or unguarded gesture was an impossibility. After I woke up from my trance on the bridge I trembled with loneliness, and in this mood I reflected on my past and my future. All sorts of things went through my mind as I clattered over the bridge in my clogs, and I began to dream again. Finally I sighed and wondered whether I would ever make my mark in the world. . . .

I really studied hard, driven on by the thought that, more than anything, I must stand out from the crowd. After I entered the third grade, I was always at the top of my class. It was difficult to stay there without being called a grind, but not only did I manage to avoid this indignity, I even succeeded in getting my classmates to perform tricks for me. No less a person than the captain of the judo club, whom we called Octopus, was one of my minions. In the corner of the classroom stood a big vase that was used for waste-paper, and if once in a while I would point to it and say, "Back into your pot now, Octopus," he would laugh and stick his head in. The echo of his laughter in the vase was eerie. I also got on well with most of the good-lookers in the class. Not one of them felt tempted to laugh at the triangular, hexagonal, and flower-shaped adhesive plasters that dotted my face to cover my pimples.

I suffered a great deal on account of these pimples. They were spreading all the time, and every morning when I woke up I would touch my face to check the situation. I tried all sorts of medicines, but none was any help. When I went to the drugstore, I would write down the name of the medicine I wanted on a scrap of paper and pretend that I was buying it for someone else. For I thought my acne was a sign that I was prey to feelings of lust, and this made me almost desperate with shame. I even seriously wished I were dead. My face caused my reputation in the family to sink to unplumbed depths. I heard that my eldest sister, who was married, had even gone so far as to say that she could hardly imagine a girl ever wanting to become my wife. I applied my medicine with renewed vigor.

My younger brother was also worried about my pimples, and he went to the drugstore I don't know how many times to buy medicine for me. My brother and I had never really got along—when he took the middle-school entrance exam I actually prayed that he would fail—but now that we were both away from home, I gradually began to appreciate his good points. As he grew up, my brother became reticent and shy. He would occasionally submit an essay for our club

7

magazine, but they were all weak-spirited efforts. He was constantly depressed because his grades were not as good as mine, but when I tried to console him he invariably ended up in even lower spirits. It troubled him too that his hairline receded into a widow's peak, which made him look a bit like a woman. He firmly believed that he was less bright because his forehead was so narrow. But for my part, this brother was the only person I trusted completely. In my relations with others I either put up my guard or laid bare my soul; it was one or the other. My brother and I had no secrets from each other.

One moonless night in early autumn we went to the pier and, refreshed by the breeze that blew in from across the straits, we discussed the case of the red thread. One day our Japanese teacher had told us in class that each of us had an invisible red thread bound around the little toe of his right foot. This thread grew longer and longer, until it fastened itself to the little toe of a girl. No matter how far apart the boy and girl might be, the thread would never break; no matter how close, even when meeting in the street, the thread would never get tangled. We were destined to marry that girl. It was the first time I had heard this story, and it so excited me that I told it to my brother as soon as I got home. We discussed it that night, the sound of the waves and the cries of the sea gulls in our ears. When I asked him what he thought his future wife was doing at that moment, he shook the railing of the pier a few times with both hands and said, coyly: "Walking in the garden." A girl, big garden clogs on her feet and a fan in her hand, looking at the evening primroses; she and my brother would make a really good pair, I thought. It was my turn to tell, but fixing my eyes on the pitch-black sea I merely said: "She's wearing a red sash," and fell silent. On the horizon the ferry from across

8

the straits swayed into sight, yellow lights blazing in countless rooms, like a big hotel.[2]

That younger brother died two or three years later, but in those days, how we loved to visit the pier. Even on snowy winter nights we would unfurl our umbrellas and go there together. What a pleasure it was to watch the snow fall silently into the deep waters of the harbor. Recently Aomori has become a bustling port, and our pier is now so busy with ships it no longer affords much of a view. The broad river that resembles Tokyo's Sumida is the Tsutsumi River, which flows through the eastern part of Aomori City and empties into Aomori Bay. Just before it joins the sea, there is one spot where the current becomes so strangely sluggish that it seems as if the river is flowing backward. I would stand there staring at the lazy current and let my mind wander. This spot symbolizes, one might say, the moment just before my youth flowed out to sea.

The four years I spent in Aomori are a time in my life I shall not easily forget, and the seaside hot spring of Asamushi, some twelve kilometers to the east, also plays a role in the same period. In "Memories" there is the following passage:

At the beginning of autumn I took my brother to a hot spring on the coast, some thirty minutes from the city by train. My mother and convalescent younger sister had rented a house there to take the waters. I stayed with them while continuing my studies for the examination. Because I enjoyed the dubious distinction of being bright, I absolutely had to show I could live up to the reputation and enter higher school after only four years in middle school. About that time my dislike of school became even more intense, but driven as I was, I took my studies seriously. Every day I boarded the train at Asamushi and went to school. My friends would visit me on Sundays, and we would invariably go off for a picnic. On the flat rocks by the sea we would cook a stew and drink wine. My brother had a good voice and knew many songs; we learned them from him and sang along. Tired out by all these amusements, we would fall asleep on the rocks, to find when we woke up that the tide had turned and the rocks, which ought to have been connected with the mainland, had become an island. We felt we were still dreaming.

Yes, the temptation to joke about my youth ebbing away into the sea is strong.

The sea at Asamushi is limpid and quite attractive, but that isn't to say the hotels are any good. The place looks like what it is—a chilly northeastern fishing village. Not that this should be held against it—it's natural enough—but am I the only one who has ever been annoyed by its odd, petty arrogance, like that of the frog in the well who knew nothing of the big ocean? Because this hot spring lies in my own native land, I feel I can say exactly what I think of it: this is the countryside, and yet there is a strange lack of the ease and naturalness one associates with the country, as if Asamushi had lost its native innocence. I have not spent the night in Asamushi for a while, but I'd be surprised if the hotel charges were not outrageously expensive.

I am of course exaggerating. The closest I've come to staying at the resort recently was when I gazed at its lodging houses through my train window. All my comments spring from the narrow-mindedness of a poor artist and from nothing else, so I must not foist these prejudices of mine on the reader. On the contrary, perhaps he had better not believe them at all. I am sure that Asamushi has made a fresh start and is now once again an unpretentious health resort. All this is merely the talk of a penniless and peevish traveling man of letters who a few times of late passed through the hot spring of his memories but did not venture off the train, and who was struck by the suspicion that exuberant young blades from Aomori may once have implanted outrageous ideas in the head of this chilly hot-spring resort, befuddling the landladies with addlebrained fantasies of how their thatched cottages rivaled the hotels of Atami and Yugawara.

Asamushi is the most famous hot spring in Tsugaru, but Ōwani, I suppose, comes second. Ōwani is situated at the foot of the mountains in the southernmost part of Tsugaru, close to the border with Akita Prefecture. It seems to be better known as a skiing resort than as a hot spring. Something of the aura of the Tsugaru clan's history still hangs over the place. As my family often went there to take the waters, I also visited Ōwani when I was a boy, but I do not remember it as vividly as I do Asamushi. While I cannot say that my recollections of Asamushi—for all their vividness—are always pleasant, my memories of Ōwani, though vague, make me quite nostalgic. Could it be the difference between the sea and the mountains? I have not visited Ōwani for close to twenty years now, but if I went, I wonder whether it wouldn't give me the same feeling as Asamushi; that it had coarsened itself by gorging on the stale leftovers of the city. But no—I can't imagine it. The roads from Tokyo to Ōwani are far worse than those to Asamushi, a fact which is, as far as I am concerned, a reason for optimism. And just next door lies the village of Ikarigaseki, which in the feudal era was a barrier station on the border between Tsugaru and Akita. Consequently the region is rich in historical landmarks and the people here still cling to the old Tsugaru way of life. No, I cannot believe that Ōwani will fall easy prey to the ways of the city. My last cause for optimism stands twelve kilometers to the north—Hirosaki Castle, its keep perfectly preserved to this day, year after year proudly displaying its robust good health among clouds of springtime cherry blossoms. I like to imagine that, were it not for Hirosaki Castle, Ōwani would probably drink itself sick on the dregs left by the city.

Hirosaki Castle. The historic center of the Tsugaru clan. Its founder, Ōura Tamenobu, backed the Tokugawa side at the Battle of Sekigahara and in 1603, when Tokugawa Ieyasu received the title of shogun from the emperor, became a vassal of the Tokugawa shogunate, with an annual revenue of forty-seven thousand *koku*.[3] He immediately began the construction of a castle and moat in Takaoka, as Hirosaki used to be called. The work was finished under the second lord of Tsugaru, Nobuhira, and the result was Hirosaki Castle. The castle has served as the stronghold of successive generations of feudal lords. Nobufusa, a relative of Nobumasa, the fourth lord, established a cadet branch in Kuroishi, and thus Tsugaru was divided between the domains of Hirosaki and Kuroishi. Nobumasa, who was known as the greatest of the "seven wise lords" of the Genroku era, added substantially to the prestige of Tsugaru, but under the seventh lord, Nobuyasu, the Hōreki famine [1755] and the Tenmei famine [1782–84] transformed the whole region into a hell for its miserable inhabitants and reduced the domain to a state of extreme poverty. But even though the future looked bleak, the eighth and ninth lords, Nobuharu and Yasuchika, applied themselves energetically to the task of restoring prosperity, and by the time of Yukitsugu, the eleventh lord, the danger was over. The feudal period came to a happy end when Yukitsugu's successor, Tsuguakira, returned his fief to the emperor, after which it was made a part of modern Aomori Prefecture. This, in a nutshell, is the history of Hirosaki Castle and Tsugaru. I intend to give a more detailed history of Tsugaru in later pages, but for now I would like to conclude this introduction to my homeland with some of my early memories of Hirosaki.

I lived in this castle town for three years, and during those years (I was enrolled in the literature department of Hirosaki Higher School) I went in for *gidayū* chanting in a big way.[4] It was an altogether peculiar affair. On my way home from school I would stop at the house of the woman who taught me *gidayū*. I can't remember what piece I learned first—perhaps the *Asagao Diary*—but I soon came to know by heart all of *Nozaki Village, Tsubosaka*, and even *The Love Suicides at Amijima*. Why did I take up this strange hobby, so out of character for me? I doubt that I can cast all the blame on Hirosaki, but I do think the city should shoulder at least part of the responsibility.

For some strange reason, *gidayū* is popular in Hirosaki. Occasionally there were amateur performances in the city theater. Once, I went to watch. The good burghers of the town, dressed punctiliously in ceremonial garb, bellowed out their parts with great zeal. What they lacked in skill, they more than made up for in the seriousness of their approach, for their style of narration was utterly unaffected and extremely conscientious. Aomori, too, has always had its fair share of aesthetes, but they, it seems, take singing lessons merely out of a desire to hear a geisha purr how clever they are. Or they are the shrewd sort, who use the status they acquire as persons of taste for political or business purposes. But respectable gentlemen who, in their sincere attempts to master some insignificant form of art, go to such absurd lengths that the sweat flows in torrents from their brows—their kind, I believe, is to be found in Hirosaki.

In short, in Hirosaki there are still real fools left. It is recorded in the seventeenth-century *Ei-Kei War Chronicle* that:

> The people of both provinces of Ōu are obstinate and do not know how to yield to those who are stronger than they are. "This man is our hereditary enemy, and that man is basely born! Only when the fortunes of war smile on him can he boast of his prowess," they say, and will not yield.

The people of Hirosaki possess that kind of foolish obstinacy that knows not how to bow down before a superior force, no matter how often they are beaten and no matter how much the stubborn defense of their proud isolation makes them the laughingstock of the world.

Because I lived here for three years, I too became very nostalgic for the old days, tried to devote myself to *gidayū*, and turned into a romantic exhibitionist of the sort described in the following passage from an old story of mine.[5] It is a humorous fabrication, to be sure, but I cannot help confessing—a little ruefully—that it conveys the general picture rather well:

It was all right as long as he just drank wine in cafés, but he soon gained enough confidence to saunter into fancy restaurants and sup with the geishas there. Our young man never thought of this as being especially immoral. He believed that a smart, raffish manner was at all times in the best of taste. After he had paid a few visits to one of the castle town's quiet old restaurants, his natural tendency to show off got the better of him again, and before long it grew out of all proportion. He had been to see *The M-Company Brawl* at the playhouse, and now he wanted to dress like the firemen in the play and sprawl on the floor of the parlor that looked out on the garden behind the restaurant. He could already hear himself drawl, "Hey doll, you're sure lookin' good today."

Excitedly he began to work on his outfit. A blue apron—he found one right away. With an old-fashioned wallet in his front pocket and a swagger in his walk, he looked a proper gangster. He also bought a cummerbund, a stiff, silk one from Hakata that squeaked when he tied it around his waist. He asked a tailor to make him an unlined summer kimono of fine striped cotton. Was he a fireman, a gambler, or a shop assistant? In the end, he could have been anything in this costume. It lacked a unifying principle. At any rate, so long as it created the impression that he was the sort of person you see portrayed on the stage, our young man was satisfied.

Because it was early summer he wore hemp sandals on his bare feet. So far so good. But suddenly a curious thought occurred to him: pants! The firemen in the play had worn long, snug, blue underpants, and he wanted a pair. "You ass!" one fireman had jeered, and when he tucked up his kimono to be able to fight better, his buttocks had been set off by pants so blue they hurt your eyes. Short underwear would never do!

In his search for those pants, our hero roamed the castle town from one end to the other, but he could not find them anywhere. Walking into a clothes store or a sandal shop to inquire, he would explain eagerly:

"Look, er, you know what plasterers wear, right? You wouldn't happen to have close-fitting blue pants like that, would you?"

But the shopkeepers would smile and shake their heads. "Oh, those . . . right now . . ."

It was quite hot and the boy was sweating profusely, but he went on looking, until finally he found a shopkeeper who gave him some good advice.

"We don't carry them, but if you go down that side street over there, you'll see a store that specializes in fire-fighting equipment. Why don't you go and try there? They may be able to help you."

"Of course! The fire brigade! How stupid of me. Now that you mention it . . . of course! You're quite right."

Greatly encouraged, he hurried into the store that had been pointed out to him. It had a whole range of pumps, and there were traditional firemen's flags as well. Somewhat overwhelmed, he plucked up his courage and asked whether they had any pants. He was promptly told they had. What he was shown was certainly a pair of blue cotton pants, but all down the length of the outside of the legs they had the thick red stripe that was the emblem of the fire brigade. Not even he had the courage to walk around in those. Sadly our hero decided that he had no option but to give up on his pants.

Even in this paradise of fools, there can have been few people as foolish as that.

While copying this passage, its author himself became a little downcast. The amusement quarter where I supped with the geishas in that fancy restaurant was, I believe, called Hackberry Alley. After some twenty years my memories have become hazy and inaccurate, but I do remember the name: Hackberry Alley, just at the foot of a slope leading up to a shrine. And the place where I wandered in my hot sweaty search for blue pants is called the Embankment, Hirosaki's busiest shopping street. Aomori's pleasure district, on the other hand, is called Beach Quarter, a name that seems to me to lack character. Aomori's equivalent of the Embankment is called the Large Quarter, and of that name I have the same opinion.

This is a good opportunity to list the names of some of the districts in Hirosaki and Aomori. It may make the difference between these two little cities unexpectedly clear. The districts in Hirosaki have names like Old Town, Administration Quarter, the Embankment, Sumiyoshi Quarter,[6] Coopers' Quarter, Coppersmiths' Quarter, Tea Plantation, Bailiff's Quarter, Reed Field, Hundred *Koku* Quarter, Upper and Lower Swordmakers' Quarters, Artillery Quarter, Subalterns' Quarter, Servants' Quarter, Falconers' Quarter, Fifty *Koku* Quarter, and Dyers' Quarter. The districts in Aomori, on the other hand, are called Beach Quarter, New Beach Quarter, Large Quarter, Rice Quarter, New Quarter, Willow Quarter, Temple Quarter, Tsutsumi Quarter, Salt Quarter, Clam Quarter, New Clam Quarter, Bay Quarter, the

Breakwater, Prosperous Quarter, and so on.

But even though its names are more interesting, I do not for a moment think Hirosaki superior to Aomori. Names that recall the past, like Falconers' or Dyers' Quarter, are by no means unique to Hirosaki—they are to be found in castle towns all over the country. Certainly, Hirosaki's Mount Iwaki is more graceful than Aomori's Mount Hakkōda, but the great Tsugaru novelist Kasai Zenzō taught the young people of his native Hirosaki: "Don't let it go to your heads. Mount Iwaki looks so beautiful because there are no high mountains around it, but go look in other parts of the country and you'll find plenty of others like it. It's such a wonderful sight only because it stands there all by itself, but don't let it go to your heads!"

Why is it that, in spite of the fact that Japan has such an abundance of historic castle towns, the people of Hirosaki appear so obstinately proud of their town's feudal character? Without being unduly harsh one may say that, compared to Kyushu, Western Honshu, or the Yamato Plain around Nara, a region like Tsugaru is but recently developed frontier country. What sort of history can it claim as its own to brag of to the rest of the nation? Even in as recent an event as the Meiji Restoration, did anyone from the Tsugaru domain actively support the imperial cause? And what was the attitude of the clan government? Did it not—to put it bluntly—just follow the lead of the other clans? Where are the traditions for Tsugaru to boast about? And yet somehow the people of Hirosaki persist in holding their heads high in the air. No matter how powerful the opponent: " 'That man is basely born! Only when the fortunes of war smile on him can he boast of his prowess,' they say, and will not yield."

I have heard it said that General Ichinohe Hyōei, who came from Hirosaki, invariably wore a kimono and a formal serge skirt on his visits to his native town. He knew that if he wore his general's uniform on those occasions, the people would immediately

17

glare at him, square their shoulders defiantly, and say, "What's he got that's so special? He's just been lucky, that's all"; and so he wisely made it a rule to remain inconspicuous whenever he went home.

Even if this anecdote is not completely true, it does seem that the people of the castle town of Hirosaki, for God knows what reason, are so proudly defiant that such stories are considered by no means implausible. And why hide it? I, too, have a streak of recalcitrance, and although it's not the only reason, still I suppose it is largely because of my mulishness that I have been unable to this day to rise above a hand-to-mouth existence in a humble row house.

A few years ago I was asked by a magazine to write "Some Words for My Homeland" and I submitted:

I love thee, I hate thee.

I have said all sorts of uncomplimentary things about Hirosaki—not out of hatred for the place, but rather as the result of some deep reflection on my own part. I am a Tsugaru man. For generations, my ancestors have tilled the land of the Tsugaru domain. I am, so to speak, of pure Tsugaru stock; that explains why I can speak ill of Tsugaru without reserve. But if people from other parts of the country were to dismiss Tsugaru because of my criticisms, I would of course feel unhappy, because, no matter what I may say, I love Tsugaru.

Hirosaki. At present the city contains more than ten thousand houses and over fifty thousand inhabitants. Hirosaki Castle and the pagoda of the Saishōin have been designated National Treasures. It is said that Tayama Katai considered Hirosaki Park in cherry-blossom time the most beautiful sight in Japan. Hirosaki houses the headquarters of the Hirosaki Army Division. Every year, between the twenty-eighth of the seventh month and the first day of the eighth month of the lunar calendar, tens of thousands of people go to worship at the inner shrine on the summit of Mount Iwaki, Tsugaru's sacred mountain, and on their way there and back the pilgrims dance through the streets of the city, which is then at its liveliest.

This is more or less the sort of thing they write in travel guides. However, I felt it would be entirely unsatisfactory to limit myself to that kind of information in describing Hirosaki, and so I recalled various experiences from my boyhood to see if I could find a livelier way of upholding Hirosaki's honor. But everything I remembered was equally trivial. I just could not do it. And now finally, shocked at all the terrible abuse I have come up with, I am at a complete loss as to what to write. I am making too much of this old capital of the Tsugaru clan. It is here that you would expect the innermost soul of us Tsugaru people to reside, but my explanation so far has failed to cast any light on the true nature of the town. And a castle keep surrounded by cherry blossoms is far from being a sight unique to Hirosaki. Aren't most castles in Japan surrounded by cherry blossoms? And does it follow that Ōwani can preserve the Tsugaru spirit simply because it is close to a castle keep set among these same cherry blossoms? I wrote just a little way back that if it were not for Hirosaki Castle, Ōwani would probably drink itself sick on the dregs left by the city, but I suppose I got carried away there. Now that I have thought everything over thoroughly, I have come to feel that this was merely an example of your author wrapping sloppy sentimentalism in purple prose, nothing more than a sign of his becoming discouraged at his inability to communicate.

Strictly speaking it is Hirosaki that is sloppy. Although it was the capital of generations of feudal lords, the prefectural office was snatched from under its nose by a newly established town. Almost

19

all the prefectural governments of Japan are situated in former feudal capitals. I firmly believe the prefecture has been ill served by the decision to make Aomori the capital, and not Hirosaki. I have absolutely nothing against Aomori. It is refreshing to see a new town prosper. All I mean to say is that it irks me to see Hirosaki accept its defeat with such indifference. It is quite natural and human to want to help someone when he is down. In my attempts to support Hirosaki, I diligently scribbled down whatever came to mind, no matter how boring, but in the last analysis I was unable to give a convincing description of Hirosaki's special charm or the unrivaled power of its castle.

I repeat. Here resides the soul of the Tsugaru people. There must be something: some unique, beautiful tradition you cannot find anywhere else in Japan, look where you may. I can definitely sense it, but to show my readers what it is, or what shape it takes, is more than I am capable of, and this troubles me beyond words. It is utterly infuriating

I remember how one spring evening, when I was a student of literature at Hirosaki Higher School, I visited the castle on my own. As I stood looking out toward Mount Iwaki from a corner of the open space in front of the main keep, I suddenly noticed a dream town silently unfolding at my feet. I felt a thrill of surprise. Until then I had always thought that Hirosaki Castle stood isolated on the outskirts of town. But look! There immediately below the castle lay a graceful old town that I had never seen until that moment, its little houses huddled together just as they had been hundreds of years ago, its breath suspended. So, I remember thinking, there's a town here, too! I felt as if I were in a dream, and, boy that I was, all of a sudden I sighed, long and deeply. It was as if I had come upon one of the ''hidden ponds'' of which the *Man'yōshū* speaks. I do not know why, but at that moment I felt as if I could understand both Hirosaki and Tsugaru. And it occurred to me that Hirosaki would never be commonplace as long as that old town was there.

There's more to it than that, however. It is because Hirosaki Castle has this "hidden pond" that it stands so exalted. My readers may not know what to make of these vain, these rash pontifications, but now that I've made them I have no choice but to insist on them. So long as the trees near the pond bear a myriad flowers and its white-walled keep stands proud and silent, Hirosaki Castle will surely rank among the great castles of the world. Nor will the hot spring nearby ever lose its untainted purity. And with this attempt at "wishful thinking," to use a modern expression, let us leave this beloved castle of mine.

When you come to think of it, trying to convey the essential nature of your native region is about as easy as trying to describe your closest relatives, that is to say, almost impossible—you do not know whether to praise them or run them down. While reviewing for this introduction to Tsugaru my boyhood memories of Kanagi, Goshogawara, Aomori, Hirosaki, Asamushi, and Ōwani, I forgot myself and came up with a whole string of vilifications, but I cannot help feeling depressed when I consider whether I have really succeeded in describing those six towns accurately. I may have offended in ways for which I deserve a thrashing. Because these towns are so intimately related to my past, because they formed my character and determined the course of my life, I am perhaps all the more incapable of looking at them without prejudice. Now that I am trying to explain them, I realize clearly that I am not at all qualified to do so. I really want to avoid writing about these places in the body of this book. Instead, I will tell you about other Tsugaru towns.

So I will go back to the words with which I began this Introduction. One spring I traveled, for the first time in my life, around the Tsugaru Peninsula in the far north of Honshu. This was really the first time I had ever visited other towns and villages in Tsugaru. Until then I was acquainted only with the six I have mentioned. While I was in elementary school, I visited a number of small villages near Kanagi on school excursions and the like, but my memories of these places are hazy at best. During my summer vacations from middle school I would return home, throw myself down on the sofa in the Western-style room on the second floor, and read whatever book was closest at hand in my elder brothers' library while guzzling soda from a bottle—I never took any trips anywhere. At higher school I invariably spent my vacations in Tokyo with one of my elder brothers (who studied sculpture but died when he was twenty-seven), and as soon as I graduated I registered at a university in Tokyo and did not return to my hometown for ten years. And so I must stress that this trip to Tsugaru was a very important event for me.

In my descriptions of the places I visited during my journey I want to avoid the knowing tone of the specialist holding forth on topography, geology, astronomy, economy, history, education, sanitation, or what have you. Wherever I do go into such things it is mere tinsel, the result of one night of embarrassingly superficial research. People who want to know more had better consult the scholars who have made special studies of the region. I have specialized in something different, something that people call love, for want of a better word. It is a field of study that examines the human heart in its relations with other hearts. On my journey, I pursued for the most part my studies in this field. But if I also manage to give my readers an idea of Tsugaru as it is today, of all aspects of life there, then perhaps this modern *Tsugaru Gazetteer* will have passed the test. Ah! If only that were within my powers. . . .

1 (p. 2) "The Dandy's Progress" ("*Oshare dōji*"), 1939.
2 (p. 9) From "Memories" ("*Omoide*"), 1933.
3 (p. 12) A *koku* is a measure of rice (180 liters, or 44.8 U.S. gallons)

used to estimate the revenue of feudal lords and the salaries of officials. This latter use is reflected in the names of two Hirosaki town quarters (see p. 16).

4 (p. 12) *Gidayū* is the name of the chanting that accompanies puppet drama performances.

5 (p. 14) "The Dandy's Progress."

6 (p. 16) *Sumiyoshi Quarter.* Location of an old shrine dedicated to the tutelary god of mariners; probably included in this list because it recalls the Tsugaru lords' traditional interest in the shipping trade.

I

A Pilgrimage

"And why," my wife asked, "are you making this trip?"

"Because things are getting me down."

"Things are always getting you down. I don't believe it for a moment."

"Masaoka Shiki, 35; Ozaki Kōyō, 36; Saitō Ryoku'u, 37; Kunikida Doppo, 37; Nagatsuka Takashi, 36; Akutagawa Ryūnosuke, 35; Kamura Isota, 36."

"What do you mean by that?"

"The age at which they all died. All the same age. Me too, I'm just about reaching that age. For an author, this is the most important time of his life."

"The time when things get him down?"

"What are you talking about? Spare me your jokes. You know very well what I mean. I won't say any more about it. If I do, it'll only sound pretentious. So—I'm going on a trip!"

Perhaps because I have lived such a feckless life up till now, it strikes me as pretentious to explain my feelings (it is also a rather hackneyed literary device), so I won't add anything more.

The editor of a publishing company, a close friend of mine, had been suggesting for some time that I write about Tsugaru, and as I too wanted, while I still had the chance, to explore my native land, every nook and cranny of it, one day in the middle of May I set out from Tokyo, looking like a tramp.

The expression "looking like a tramp" is perhaps a bit too subjective, but even objectively speaking I did not cut a very fine figure. I had not a single suit in my possession, only the work clothes of the labor service,[1] and these were not exactly custom-made. My wife had sewn them out of some cotton cloth we had lying around which she had first dyed navy blue and then fashioned into something approaching a jumper and a pair of trousers, but of an unusual, puzzling shape. They were indeed navy blue right after she dyed them, but after I had worn them out of doors once or twice, they abruptly changed color and turned a strange, purplish hue. And purple clothes do not look right even on a woman, unless she is very beautiful. With these purple work clothes I wore green rayon puttees and white canvas shoes with rubber soles. My hat was a rayon tennis cap. For this old dandy it was quite unprecedented to set out on a journey dressed like that, but true to form I had tucked into my rucksack an unlined formal jacket with the family crest embroidered on it and a lined kimono of fine handspun silk, both of which had been made by altering clothes left me as a memento by my mother. I also carried a formal skirt of high-quality silk. One never knows when such things may come in handy.

I boarded the 5:30 P.M. ordinary express from Ueno Station in Tokyo. As the night wore on, it became bitterly cold. Under my so-called jumper I had on nothing but two thin shirts, and under my trousers only shorts. Even people who had taken the precaution of wearing an overcoat or bringing along a rug to spread over their legs were grumbling.

"Cold! Why does it have to be so cold tonight!"

I had not expected it to be so cold either. In Tokyo some rash souls were already walking around in only one layer of serge clothing. I had forgotten how cold it could be in the north. I pulled in my hands and feet as far as I could, until I looked like a turtle in its shell, and tried to tell myself that this was the way to purify my mind of worldly thoughts. But as dawn broke

25

it became still colder, so I abandoned my attempts at purification and was reduced to a state of banality in which all I could do was pray ardently for the fulfillment of the utterly mundane desire to arrive in Aomori quickly so that I could stretch out at the fireside of some inn and have a drink of hot *sake*.

We arrived in Aomori at eight o'clock in the morning. T. had come to the station to meet me. I had written him a letter to tell him I was coming.

"I thought you'd be wearing a kimono."

"That would hardly be in keeping with the times," I said, making an effort to be funny.

T. had his little girl with him, and I immediately regretted not having brought a present for her.

"How about stopping at my house to take a rest?"

"Thanks, but I was thinking of reaching N.'s place in Kanita by noon."

"I know. He told me. He's expecting you. But why not rest a while at my house until the bus for Kanita leaves?"

My disgracefully vulgar wish to stretch out at the fireside and have a drink of hot *sake* was miraculously fulfilled. In T.'s house the sunken hearth was filled with blazing charcoal, and the iron kettle hanging over it contained a small bottle of *sake*.

"You must be exhausted after your journey." T. bowed to me in formal welcome. "Perhaps you'd rather have some beer?"

"No, *sake* is fine," I said, coughing lightly.

T. used to be one of our family servants, and his main task had been to look after the poultry. Because we were the same age, we had a lot of fun playing together. "Scolding the maids: that's his strength and his weakness," was, I remember, how my grandmother summed him up. Later he left us to study in Aomori and found a job in a hospital, where he appears to have won the trust of patients and staff alike. A few years ago he left for the front and fought on some lonely island in the south, but he fell

26

ill and was repatriated last year, and is now, after recovering from his illness, working in his old hospital again.

"What was it you enjoyed most at the front?"

"The moment," T. answered promptly, "when we were given our one-cup ration of beer. I would savor the beer slowly, relishing every sip, and always meaning to part cup from lips for a breather halfway through, but never managing to do so."

T. used to be a big drinker, but he has given it up completely. And from time to time he coughs quietly.

"So how are you feeling now?" A long time ago he had had lung trouble, and it had acted up again at the front.

"From now on it's the home front for me. If you haven't yourself suffered at some stage from illness, you can't fully understand how to take care of hospital patients. It's been a good experience for me."

"It's really rounded you out, hasn't it? But actually, those chest problems of yours . . ." I had become a bit drunk and without compunction began to explain medical matters to a doctor. "It's all psychological. Once you stop thinking about it, it'll go away. Just drink your fill, once in a while."

"Yes, well . . . I try not to overdo things," he said, laughing. It seems the expert had little faith in my wild medical theories. "But won't you have something to eat? Though I'm afraid these days good fish has become scarce, even in Aomori."

"No, thanks." I gazed indifferently at the tray beside me. "It all looks delicious. Sorry to have troubled you so. But I'm really not hungry."

Before setting out for Tsugaru, I had made one secret resolution, and that was to stop caring about food. I am no saint myself, so I shouldn't be talking, but the people of Tokyo care far too much about filling their bellies. Maybe I am just old-fashioned, for though it strikes me as quite funny, I love that sort of foolish, almost masochistic sham indifference epitomized by the samurai with empty stomach picking his teeth as if he had just eaten. You may think it unnecessary to go so far as to use toothpicks, but this is how a man shows his mettle. And a man's mettle tends to show itself in funny ways.

I have heard that there are people in Tokyo quite lacking in moral fiber, who go off into the country and complain in greatly exaggerated terms of their sad plight and how they are on the brink of starvation, and as they reverently eat the white rice offered them by the country folk, they petition for more—their faces wreathed in servile smiles and their mouths oozing compliments all the while.[2] "Might I perhaps ask for some more food? Ah, you have potatoes? How kind of you! How many months has it been since I last ate such delicious potatoes! Oh, and by the way, I would like to take some home with me. Would you perhaps be kind enough to give me some?" Everyone in Tokyo should be getting fixed and equal portions rationed out to him. It is very odd, therefore, that any one person should be that much closer to starvation than any other. Perhaps they suffer from gastric expansion. Nevertheless, it is disgraceful to bow and scrape for food. I do not intend to play judge and remind these people it is all for the sake of our country, but I do believe that one should at all times preserve one's dignity as a human being.

I have also heard it said that because of these few exceptional cases of Tokyo people going into the country with totally groundless complaints about a food shortage in the capital, country people have come to regard visitors from Tokyo with scorn, thinking they have all come to hunt for food. Thus it was in part for the good name of all the people of Tokyo that I went to Tsugaru with the secret resolution to proclaim defiantly to all and sundry: "I have not come to Tsugaru to scrounge food! I may look like a beggar clad in purple, but I am begging for truth and love, not for white rice!" Even if someone were to say to me, with all the kindness of his heart, "Come! Have some white rice. Eat until your stomach bursts. Things are terrible in Tokyo, I'm told," I was going to eat no more than one bowl and then say: "Maybe it's a question of habit, but I think the rice in Tokyo tastes better. As for other food, just when we're about to run out, in come the rations. My stomach shrank before I knew it; a little food is enough to fill me up now. No problem at all!"

It turned out, however, that this somewhat perverse resolution served no purpose at all. I visited the homes of acquaintances all over Tsugaru, but not one of them said to me: "Here's some white rice for you. Stuff it all in, please do, until your belly bursts!" Even my eighty-eight-year-old grandmother in my own home told me, embarrassed: "In Tokyo you can get all the delicacies you want, so we racked our brains thinking up something good to serve you. I wanted to make you cucumbers pickled in *sake*, but—I don't know why—these days it's absolutely impossible to get *sake* lees for the pickling." I felt I was really fortunate. I thanked the gods for my good luck. Nor was there anyone who insisted on loading me with presents of food to take home, with a "please take this," and a "please take that." As a result, I was able to proceed with a light heart and a light rucksack. But when I returned to Tokyo, I was amazed to find awaiting me at home lots of packages sent me by the kind people of the various places I had visited.

But to return to my story: T. did not press any food on me either, and the question of the food situation in Tokyo never cropped up in our conversation. For the most part we reminisced about the days we spent playing together in my Kanagi home.

"You know, I consider you a true friend." These are really rude, uncouth, and pretentious words, swollen with a disagreeable theatricality. I squirmed as soon as they escaped my lips. Are there no other ways of saying this?

"I'm not too happy to hear you say so." T. also seemed sensitive in this respect. "I am just someone who used to work in your house at Kanagi, and you are still my master. I won't have

29

you think of it any other way. It's strange, isn't it? Twenty years have passed, but even nowadays I often dream of your Kanagi house. Even at the front, many was the time I woke up with a start, thinking, 'Damn it! I forgot to feed the chickens.' ''

It was time for the bus. T. and I went out together. I was not cold any more. Far from it—the weather was nice, I had drunk hot *sake*, and instead of being cold I felt my forehead dripping with sweat. The cherry blossoms in Gappo Park were in full bloom. The streets of Aomori were dusty white and dry. . . . But I must be careful not to relate the hazy impression they made on my *sake*-blurred eyes, for Aomori is now involved in a giant shipbuilding effort. On the way we visited the grave of old Mr. Toyoda, who had been so kind to me while I was at middle school, and then hurried on to the bus station.

In the old days I would not have hesitated to ask T.: ''How about it? Won't you come along to Kanita with me?'' But perhaps because I am older now I have learned to be more reserved, or perhaps . . . No, let's not have any complicated explanations of my feelings. After all, isn't it just that we had both grown up? Grown-ups are lonely people. Even if we love each other, we must be careful not to show it publicly. And why all this caution? The answer is simple: because people are too often betrayed and put to public shame. The discovery that you cannot trust people is the first lesson young people learn as they grow up into adults. Adults are adolescents who have been betrayed. I kept my mouth shut. It was T. who suddenly spoke up.

''I'll take the first bus to Kanita tomorrow morning. I'll see you again at N.'s.''

''But what about the hospital?''

''Tomorrow is Sunday.''

''So it is! Why didn't you say so earlier?''

Deep in our hearts we were still young boys.

1 (p. 25) *Labor service.* A voluntary civilian enlistment program. According to a 1940 dress ordinance, all Japanese civilian men had to wear khaki uniforms, and in 1944 a field service cap and puttees were added. Dazai did not own such a uniform and had to travel in workman's clothes to avoid questioning by the police, though the incongruous tennis cap may have raised some eyebrows (see Sōma, p. 210).

2 (p. 28) *White rice.* In times of famine, white rice was considered a great luxury. During World War II it was replaced by more nutritious, but less tasty substitutes like unhulled rice or millet.

II

Kanita

The eastern coast of the Tsugaru Peninsula, known since ancient days as Sotogahama, the Outer Shore, was once the scene of a flourishing coastal trade. The bus from Aomori up the coast passes through Ushirogata, Yomogita, Kanita, Tairadate, Ippongi, Ima-betsu, and other towns and villages as far as Minmaya, famous from the legend of Yoshitsune. The ride takes about four hours. The bus goes no further than Minmaya, but if the traveler walks for another three hours up the lonely road that leads from Min-maya along the coast, he will finally reach the hamlet of Tappi, which stands literally at the end of the road. This promontory forms the northernmost extremity of Honshu. Because the area has recently taken on considerable importance for reasons of na-tional security, I must avoid a more detailed description and can give only a vague idea of the distances involved. But what I can say is that the Sotogahama region has the longest history of any part of Tsugaru, and that Kanita is its biggest community. The bus from Aomori passes through Ushirogata and Yomogita and reaches Kanita in about an hour and a half, or perhaps nearer two hours.

This is the center, so to speak, of Sotogahama. There are close to a thousand houses in Kanita, and the population appears to be well over five thousand. The Kanita police station, which I am told was finished but a little while ago, is probably one of the grandest and most conspicuous buildings in the whole region.

Kanita, Yomogita, Tairadate, Ippongi, Minmaya—in short, all the villages of Sotogahama—fall under its jurisdiction. According to the *History of Aomori Prefecture* by the Hirosaki scholar Takeuchi Unpei, Kanita's beaches used to yield iron sand, and although there is none at all left now, it is said that in the first decade of the seventeenth century this sand was smelted and its iron used in the construction of Hirosaki Castle. He also writes that five big ships were built at Kanita as part of preparations to suppress the Ainu rebellion of 1669, and that in the 1690s Nobumasa, the fourth lord of Tsugaru, designated it one of the Nine Ports of Tsugaru and appointed a commissioner whose main responsibility was to supervise the export of timber.

But these are all things I looked into later. At the time of my trip I knew only that Kanita, Crab Paddy, is famous for its crabs and that N., my closest friend at middle school, lives there. I had written him a letter saying that on my Tsugaru pilgrimage I would like to stay at his place. "Please don't go to any trouble," I think I wrote. "Just pretend I'm not there. Whatever you do, don't bother coming to meet me or anything like that. But if you could get some cider, and some crab. . . ." My self-imposed rule to stop caring about food contained an escape clause for crab. I love crab. I don't know why, but I do. Crab, shrimp, squilla, I like only light fare. And then there's another thing I'm very fond of, and that's alcohol. Ah! No sooner are we on the subject of eating and drinking than the apostle of love and truth, who was supposed not to give a damn about such things, reveals a glimpse of his inborn gluttony.

N. was waiting for me at his home, a small mountain of crab piled up on a large, low, red-lacquered table with curved legs.

"Are you sure you want only cider? Don't you want any *sake* or beer?" he asked with some hesitation.

Not want it? *Sake* and beer would certainly be a whole sight better than cider, but because I, as an "adult," knew how precious they were, I had restrained myself and mentioned only cider in my letter. I had heard that nowadays cider in Tsugaru is produced on the same scale as wine in Kōshū.

"Eh? Oh, well, whatever . . ." I smiled ambiguously.

Relief spread over N.'s face. "Ah, that makes me feel a lot better. I can't help it, but I just don't like cider. In fact, when she saw your letter, my wife went on about how you must be fed up with drinking *sake* and beer there in Tokyo and wanted to try cider because it would remind you of your hometown. That's what she thought you'd written, and that's what you were going to get. But I told her: 'I can't believe it. I just can't believe he doesn't like beer and *sake* any more. It's quite unlike him. If you ask me, I think he's just being polite.' "

"Still, your wife wasn't completely wrong."

"What are you talking about? Enough of that nonsense. Which will you have first? *Sake* or beer?"

"Let's have the beer later." I had begun to feel at home.

"I'm with you there. *Sake*, woman, bring the *sake*! It doesn't matter if it isn't quite hot yet, just bring it as quick as you can."

> Wine—wherever we may be, so hard to do without.
> Recalling our old friendship, deep in the countryside,
> We find the dreams of our green youth gone up in smoke
> And wonder at the silver in each other's hair.
> Parted twenty years ago, a million miles apart
> We were, and could we now without a glass of wine
> Relate the details of our humdrum lives?
>
> Po Chü-i

I never visited the homes of other boys while I was at middle school, but for some reason I did go to my classmate N.'s place quite often. He had lodgings on the second floor of a big liquor store in Teramachi. Every morning we would wait for each other and go to school together, and on our way back we would stroll

34

down the back street by the sea. Even when it rained we wouldn't rush or hurry, but, soaked to the skin like two drowned rats, we would walk calmly on without letting it bother us. When I think about it now, we must have seemed strange kids—neither of us could have cared less about such trifling matters. Maybe that was the key to our friendship. We would run or play tennis in the open space in front of the temple, and on Sundays we would take our lunch and go for a picnic in the mountains nearby. The character I refer to as "my friend" in "Memories" is based largely on N.

After graduating from middle school N. went to Tokyo and, I believe, worked for a company that published magazines. I left for Tokyo two or three years later to register at university, and we resumed our friendship. N. was boarding in Ikebukuro while I was at Takadanobaba, but we managed to get together almost every day. Now our recreation no longer consisted of running or tennis. N. had quit the publishing house and was working for an insurance company, but because he had this sort of lordly indifference toward the meaner things in life, he was always being cheated by people. He was just like me, but every time someone deceived me I turned a little gloomier and sneakier, whereas N. was the opposite: no matter how often he was cheated, he became more and more cheerful and easygoing. Even his rowdy friends, to a man, expressed their respect for his gentle nature.

"N.'s a funny fellow. You've got to admire the way he never lets things make him bitter. He must have inherited a store of virtue from his ancestors. How else could you explain it?"

When we were still at middle school, N. occasionally came to visit me in Kanagi, and after he had moved to Tokyo he often went to see one of my older brothers who was living in Totsuka. And when that brother died at the age of twenty-seven, N. took some days off from work and helped us in all sorts of ways, thereby earning the deep gratitude of all my relatives.

In due course N. had to come back home to take over his family's rice refinery in the country. And once he had inherited the family business, his extraordinary natural goodness gained him the trust of the young people of Kanita and got him elected to the town council a few years ago. He holds several posts, such as branch chairman of the Young Men's Association and secretary of this or that organization, so that now it seems Kanita cannot get along without him.

That night, too, several locally prominent young men visited his home. They joined us for some *sake* and beer, and N.—his popularity something quite remarkable—was of course the star of the party.

Bashō left behind a work we now know as *Precepts for Pilgrims*, and one of his precepts is: "Do not drink just because you like drinking. At parties it may be hard to refuse, but be sure to stop while you are still only slightly inebriated. And never become riotous." But because there is a line in the *Analects* of Confucius which I take to mean "Drink as much as you like, but commit no breach of manners," I ventured not to follow the old poet's advice. Even if you get totally plastered, it is all right so long as you preserve the rules of etiquette. And is that not a matter of course? I can hold my liquor—far better, I imagine, than ever Bashō could—and I trust I am not the kind of idiot who enjoys someone's hospitality only to turn riotous.

> . . . And could we now without a glass of wine
> Relate the details of our humdrum lives?

I drank a lot.

Now, among the old poet's precepts there is, it seems, another one that states: "Restrict yourself to the composition of poetry and do not indulge in small talk. If the conversation turns to other topics, take a nap to save your strength." I did not observe this precept either. Bashō presided over so many poetry-composition parties and opened so many local chapters of his school of poetry, that to us laymen it begins to look suspiciously as if his pilgrimages were really business trips to advertise the Bashō school in the provinces. Is it not selfish for a speaker, even when surrounded by an audience that came primarily to listen to his poetry, to avoid other topics altogether and to pretend to take a nap when they do come up? My journey was definitely not undertaken for the purpose of founding local chapters of the Dazai school, and of course N. had not organized this party with the idea of having me give a lecture on literature. And as for the people who had come to visit him that night, they made me feel welcome and exchanged *sake* cups with me because I was an old, close friend of N.'s. It would not have been very proper if I had repaid them with some boring lecture on ''The Whereabouts of the Spirit of Literature,'' and then propped myself up against the alcove pillar and pretended to sleep if the conversation turned to other topics.

Not once that evening did I mention the subject of literature. I did not even use the Tokyo dialect, but went to the other extreme. My efforts to speak pure Tsugaru dialect bordered on affectation. And we discussed nothing but trivial, everyday affairs. I was trying so hard to play the part of the *ozukasu*, the runt of the Tsugaru Tsushima family, that some of the other guests must have felt I didn't have to go to quite such lengths. (Tsushima Shūji is the name under which I was registered at birth. As for the word *ozukasu*, it seems more than likely that it is a dialect version of *oji kasu*, ''uncle dregs.'' It is used in this region to refer, somewhat unflatteringly, to the third or fourth son of a family.)

I must admit that I was making this journey partly to become the Tsushima runt once more. Not sure of myself as a man of the city, I hoped to find my true identity in Tsugaru. In other words, I went to see with my own eyes what the Tsugaru people

37

were really like, to look for an archetypal Tsugaru person after whom I could pattern my life. And I discovered him, so very easily, wherever I looked.

It is not really a matter of whom or how. A penniless traveler looking like a beggar is not in a position to make presumptuous comments. Indeed, it would be highly impertinent of him. It was certainly not as if I discovered my model in any one person's words or actions, or in his treatment of me. I trust I did not travel around spying on everybody I met, like some sort of detective. I usually walked with my head down, eyes fixed on the ground at my feet, but so often it happened that I heard things whispered in my ears, things that I can only regard as being part of my destiny. These things I believed.

Thus there is neither rhyme nor reason to my discoveries—they're wretchedly subjective. As to who did what, or who said what, I really didn't bother too much about that sort of thing. Which is just as it should be, for people like me are not entitled to bother, and anyway, I was not in the least concerned with reality. "Reality is in the things one believes, but reality can never make one believe." Twice over I wrote these strange words in my travel diary.

I had meant to restrain myself—but I've expressed my confused thoughts after all. My theories are so muddled that I myself often cannot understand what I am saying. There are even times when I lie. That's why I hate explaining my feelings. It seems as if this is all some sort of transparent charade I'm perpetrating, and that idea is a thoroughly humiliating one. Though I know I will regret it bitterly afterward, when I get excited I just "flog my unwilling tongue," as they say, and in a sharp voice blurt out all sorts of inconsistencies, filling my audience not so much with scorn as with pity. This seems to be my sorry fate.

But that evening I did not vent such clumsy ideas, and although it violated Bashō's instructions to posterity, I stayed awake, enjoyed nothing but small talk, and drank until very late with a pile of crab, that favorite food of mine, right in front of my eyes. N.'s wife, a small woman, always on her toes, noticed that I was having my fill just looking at the crab without actually doing anything about it, and must have thought that I considered it too much of a bother to crack the shells and pick the meat, for she briskly set to and did it for me with great skill, heaping the delicious white meat on the shells. She kept pressing more on me. Perhaps these crabs had been caught on the Kanita beach that very morning; they had the fresh, light taste of newly picked fruit. I was reminded of those fragrant cool jellies that are shaped like real fruits. Coolly violating my self-imposed rule of indifference to food, I ate a third and then a fourth.

Mrs. N. had prepared a tray for every guest that night, and even the local people were quite surprised at the abundance of the food. After the guests had left, N. and I moved the party from the parlor to the living room and began the *atofuki*, the mopping-up. In Tsugaru this term refers to something that takes place after an occasion, festive or otherwise, for which many people gather at a house. After all the guests leave, a small number of close friends and relatives collect the leftovers and have a small party in recognition of all their hard work. Perhaps *atofuki* is the dialect pronunciation of the standard *atohiki*, which means "tossing them down." But as N. could hold his liquor even better than I, there was little danger of our becoming "riotous."

"Ah," I heaved a deep sigh. "You can still drink like you used to. But after all, it was you who taught me, so it's only to be expected. . . ."

It had indeed been N. who had taught me to drink. This is an incontestable fact.

"Mmmm," N. nodded gravely, his cup in his hand. "I must admit I've thought a lot about that. Every time you got drunk and made a fool of yourself, I felt responsible, and it was hard for me. But these days I'm doing my best to get over that notion. I keep telling myself that you'd have discovered the bottle just the same without me and that it's not really something I should worry about."

"Oh yes, quite so. You're right. You aren't responsible. You're absolutely right."

Soon N.'s wife joined us, and while we were having an intimate mopping-up telling one another about our children, a cock suddenly announced the break of day, and highly surprised I went off to bed.

No sooner had I awoken next morning than I heard T.'s voice. True to his promise he had taken the first bus from Aomori. I jumped out of bed right away. When T. is around I somehow feel secure and self-confident. He had brought with him one of his colleagues at the hospital in Aomori, Mr. H., who was interested in literature. The chief administrator of the Kanita branch of their hospital, a Mr. S., had come too. And as I was washing my face, a Mr. M. arrived from Imabetsu, near Minmaya. He was a young man with a diffident smile, also interested in literature; N. must have told him that I was visiting Kanita. He appeared to be an old acquaintance of the others. They had already put their heads together and decided that we should all leave right away for a hill near Kanita to view the cherry blossoms.

Kanran Hill. I left the house wearing my purple jumper and green puttees, but there had been no need at all to dress so elaborately. Kanran Hill stands just outside the town and is less than a hundred meters high, but the view from the top that day was not at all bad. It was dazzling bright and clear, without a breath of wind. We could see Cape Natsudomari across Aomori Bay, and the Shimokita Peninsula beyond the Tairadate Straits appeared very close. People from the south may have the impression that the waters around the north of Honshu are a deep, dark, dangerous expanse of mountainous billows, but the sea near Kanita is very calm and pale. Its salt content is very low; even the rocks on the beach hardly smell of salt. It is a sea of melted snow—a lake could not be more serene. As it concerns our national security, I had perhaps better say nothing more about its depth and suchlike matters except that its waves frolic gently on a sandy beach.

The countless nets set close to the shore catch an abundance of fish in every season of the year: crab, of course, but also squid, sole, mackerel, sardines, cod, and anglerfish. In the town, now as in the past, the fishmongers pile up the fish in their bicycle carts every morning and peddle their wares in the streets, roaring at the top of their voices, as if in anger: "Squid and mackerel, yaaah! Angler and sole, yaaah! Sea bass and haddock, yaaah!" It seems the fishmongers around here only sell fish caught on the very same day and never offer any they were unable to get rid of the day before. I suppose they ship those elsewhere. That's why the people of this town eat only fish that were still alive and swimming in the morning. But it takes only one day when there is no catch—because, perhaps, the sea is too rough—and you will not find one fresh fish in the whole town. Then the people make do with dried fish and wild vegetables. This applies not just to Kanita but to all the fishing villages of Sotogahama, and to those on the west coast of Tsugaru as well.

Kanita is also well endowed with wild vegetables, for not only does it lie by the sea, but it has mountains and a plain. Because the mountains on the east coast of the peninsula drop directly into the sea, the whole region is poor in flat land, and there are many places where new rice fields and vegetable patches have been carved out of the slopes. One can well imagine, therefore, that it is not without a touch of compassion that the people who live across the mountains, on the wide Tsugaru Plain in the western part of the peninsula, refer to the Sotogahama region as the *kage*, the dark side (because it lies in the shade of the mountains). Only around Kanita will you see splendid, fertile fields, as fine as any in the plain. If they knew they were being pitied by their western neighbors, the people of Kanita would think it a good joke. In the basin of the Kanita River, a placid and well-filled stream that winds its way through the region, lie broad rice paddies and vegetable fields. While it is true that poor harvests are not uncommon because of the strong winds that blow from both east and west, the soil is not as bad as the people in the west imagine. As seen from Kanran Hill, the bountiful Kanita River twists and turns on its way like a large snake. On either side the flooded rice fields, their first plowing just finished, lie serene and withdrawn, a lush and pleasant view.

The mountains are the Bonju Mountains, a spur of the Ōu Range. They begin in the southern part of the peninsula and march directly toward Cape Tappi at the extreme north, where they drop off into the sea. They form a low range, with an average height of not more than two or three, perhaps four hundred meters. Due west of Kanran Hill towers the blue mass of Mount Ōgura, which along with Mount Masugawa is one of the highest peaks in the range, and even then I am not certain whether it reaches the seven-hundred-meter level. Of course there are some prosaic, utilitarian spirits who will rush to the defense by bringing up the old saw that a mountain is not valued because of its height but its trees. But as tired as this argument may be, it is a fact that the Tsugaru people have little reason to be ashamed of the low height of their mountains, for they contain some of the most important arborvitae forests in the country.

Yes, I say arborvitae, not apples. Apples only came to Tsugaru in the early 1870s, when seeds received from an American were planted experimentally. Sometime around 1890, French pruning methods, learned from a French missionary, resulted in such prompt success that the people of the region began to take the cultivation of apples seriously, but apples did not become nationally known as an Aomori specialty until the second decade of this century. While they are not in the same lightweight league as Tokyo's "thunder crackers"[1] or Kuwana's grilled clams, their history is shorter by far than that of the mandarins of Kishū. When you mention Tsugaru, people from Tokyo or Osaka immediately think of apples, but they seem to know very little about its forests of arborvitae. Yet the trees on the Tsugaru mountains intertwine their branches so densely and are of such a glorious blue-green, even in winter, that one may well suppose they gave their name to the prefecture: Aomori, Blue Forest.

Since ancient times the Tsugaru arborvitae forest has been regarded as one of the three great forests of Japan. The 1929 edition of the *Outline of the Geography and Customs of Japan* contains the following passage:

> The great forests of Tsugaru were first planted by the founder of the Tsugaru clan, Lord Tamenobu. After his death, a continuing policy of strict management ensured the survival of their gloomy splendor until this day. They are known throughout the nation as a model of forest management. Several miles of sand dune along the Japan Sea coast of the Tsugaru Peninsula were afforested in the 1680s to form a protective wall against the sea wind and also as part of the reclamation of the wasteland along the lower reaches of the Iwaki River. The clan government continued this project, and at the beginning of the eighteenth century the result of its energetic forestation policy could be seen in the full-grown trees of the so-called Screen Forest, which in turn contributed to the opening up of over eighty-three hundred hectares of new arable land. Intensive forestation continued everywhere within the clan territory, so that finally there were over one hundred big domanial forests. In the latter half of the nineteenth century the authorities continued to

43

pay great attention to the management of these forests, and now the quality of the arborvitae forests of Aomori is known everywhere. The timber of this region is perhaps most valued because of its eminent suitability for all sorts of building purposes; it is especially resistant to humidity, is produced in abundant quantities, and can be transported comparatively easily. The yearly production is 144 metric tons.

As this was written in 1929, I assume that the present production levels are about three times as high. This account refers to the arborvitae forests of all Tsugaru and cannot be used to extol those of Kanita alone, but it is a fact that the densely wooded mountains one can see from Kanran Hill contain the most splendid forest in Tsugaru. In the *Outline* there is also a large photograph of the mouth of the Kanita River, with the following explanation:

Near the Kanita River stands a state-owned forest of arborvitae, one of the three most beautiful forests in Japan. The timber is shipped from Kanita, a port that bustles with activity. A special forestry railroad leads from the coast here into the mountains; every day great quantities of timber are transported along it to the harbor. The timber from this region is well known not only for its quality but also for its low price.

I suppose it is natural for the people of Kanita to be proud of their town.

The Bonju Mountains, which form the backbone of the Tsugaru Peninsula, have forests of cedar, beech, oak, *katsura*, horse chestnut, and larch in addition to the arborvitae, as well as an abundance of wild vegetables. In Kanagi across the mountains, too, wild vegetables grow in great quantities, but here in Kanita bracken, osmunds, spikenard, bamboo shoots, coltsfoot, thistles, and all sorts of mushrooms can be gathered in the foothills close to town.

Thus Kanita, with its rice paddies and vegetable fields, blessed with products of land and sea, may appear to my readers as a land of Cockaigne in which the people live in perfect peace and happiness, but as it lay there at the bottom of Kanran Hill, there seemed to be something sluggish about Kanita. It lacked vigor.

I have written only good things about Kanita thus far (too many almost), so I will assume its people will bear with me if my comments take a more critical turn. The Kanita people are good-natured—a great virtue, to be sure, but to the traveler the town seems almost depressing because this good-naturedness borders on lethargy. Kanita is so perfectly still, so deadly quiet, that it makes you wonder if its many natural blessings may not have had an adverse influence. The breakwater at the mouth of the river looks as if it was abandoned half-complete. Ground has been leveled to build a house, but then the house has not been built and there in the red clay they have planted pumpkins. Not that you can see all that from Kanran Hill, but it seems to me that in Kanita too many building projects are abandoned before they are finished.

I asked N. if the town's healthy progress was perhaps being obstructed by the machinations of some old fogies, but the young councillor merely forced a smile and told me to drop the subject. Samurai should not do business, and writers should not talk politics. My impertinent question about the way Kanita was run merely invited a pitying look from the professional politician, and I was left feeling pretty silly.

This reminds me of the story of a gaffe committed by another artist. In a corridor of a theater in Paris, the famous French painter Edgar Degas once found himself sharing a sofa with the great statesman Clemenceau. Degas was not at all taken aback, but turned to the politician and gave a noble speech espousing his long-held convictions on the life political: ''If I were prime minister, in consideration of my heavy responsibilities I would sever all bonds of love and affection. I would choose a life as plain and simple as an ascetic's. I would rent a tiny little room on the fifth floor of an apartment building in the immediate vicinity of my office. It would have nothing more than a table and a simple iron bed, and when I came home from my office, I would work at that table till deep into the night to get the day's unfinished business out of the way. When overcome with sleep, I would not even take off my clothes and shoes but just fall down on the bed, and on opening my eyes the next morning I would jump up right away, snatch a breakfast of soup and an egg on my feet, slip my briefcase under my arm, and go to my office.'' He spoke with great passion, but Clemenceau answered not a word and only stared the famous painter in the face with eyes that betrayed his utter disgust and contempt. Degas was destroyed by that stare. Deeply ashamed, he never mentioned this blunder to a soul. Only after fifteen years did he unburden himself, in deepest secret, to Valéry, who seems to have been the closest of his few friends.

Considering that he did his utmost to conceal this episode for fifteen years—an excruciatingly long time—the haughty, arrogant painter must have felt to the very marrow of his bones his defeat before the withering stare leveled at him, unconsciously, by the seasoned politician. I cannot help but feel an outpouring of sympathy for him. When artists talk politics, they are likely to get hurt. Degas illustrates this beautifully. For me, a mere writer without a penny in his pocket, the safest course seems to be to limit myself to the cherry blossoms on Kanran Hill and the affection of my Tsugaru friends.

The previous day a strong westerly wind had been rattling the sliding doors of N.'s house, and with my gift for jumping to conclusions I had volunteered the inspired opinion that Kanita really is a windy town, but today, as if laughing up its sleeve at my rash remarks of the night before, Kanita had presented us with beautiful, calm weather. There was not a breath of wind. The cherry blossoms of Kanran Hill appeared to be at their best now. Peacefully they bloomed, delicate and transitory. To describe them as luxuriant would be wrong. Their petals faintly transparent, they were almost forlorn, as if cleansed by the snow. They seemed to belong to some different species of cherry. So delicate were their colors that I wondered whether Novalis had not perhaps envisioned just such blossoms when he described his "blue flower."[2]

We sat down on the grass under the blossoms and opened our lunch boxes. You could see that the food had been prepared by N.'s wife. Apart from the boxes, there was a big bamboo hamper with lots of crabs and squillas. And then, beer. I tried not to look too greedy as I peeled the squillas, sucked the crab legs, and applied my chopsticks to the food in the boxes. There was squid that had been stuffed with its own transparent roe, then broiled in soy sauce and cut into round slices; of all the food in the boxes, this was the most tormentingly delicious. T., the repatriated soldier, complained about the heat and took off his shirt. He stood up and, half-naked, began to do army-style calisthenics. With a hand towel for a headband, his swarthy face looked a little like that of Burma's head of state, Ba Maw.

Although there were varying degrees of enthusiasm for the idea, there seemed to be some consensus among the group that they would like me to tell them something of my thoughts concerning the present state of the novel. I gave clear answers to the questions I was asked. This was according to Bashō's dictum "It is not seemly to fail to answer a question," but I completely ignored other, much more important precepts: "Do not blame the mote in the eyes of others, while ignoring the beam in your own," and, "It is exceedingly base to slander others but to praise oneself." That exceedingly base act I committed. To be sure, even Bashō occasionally took swipes at the poems of other schools, but I don't think he ever sank to the despicable depths I did—denouncing other writers so shamelessly, eyebrows screwed up, mouth dis-

47

torted, shoulders hunched in scorn. Disgusting though it must have been, this was just the kind of disgraceful behavior I displayed.

When asked about the work of a Japanese author who is now in his fifties, I dismissed it with a brusque, "Not that good."[3] Recently, the earlier work of this writer has for some reason been acclaimed with feelings bordering on idolatry even by readers in Tokyo. Some people have gone so far as to call him a god. It's all the rage to say you like this novelist; it testifies to your refined taste. But I suppose the writer himself watches this strange vogue with a great deal of barely concealed annoyance, for it really does him no service. I had been observing his curious influence from a distance and was fuming in solitary anger while in that asinine Tsugaru way of mine I muttered, "That man is basely born! Only when the fortunes of war . . . ," etc., etc. I was not about to jump on the bandwagon.

A while ago, when I tried to read his work again, I thought, "Well done!" but I found little in it that I could call refined. On the contrary, I even wondered if his strength might not lie in vulgarity. The world he describes is that of the meaningless, pretentious joys and sorrows of the penny-pinching lower-middle classes. His main characters sometimes reflect "piously" on their way of living, but these passages are so stale one tends to think that if he had to make their reflections that dull he would have done better not to put them in at all. I feel a pettiness, as if in his attempts to grow out of his literary immaturity he had entrapped himself in this kind of writing. There are also passages that were apparently meant to be humorous, more such passages than one would expect, but there is a timorous and mediocre streak in them—the result perhaps of excessive self-consciousness—which prevents his readers from laughing heartily.

Some have called him "aristocratic," but this strikes me as infantile. Nothing could be further from the truth, and again, it does him no service to call him so. The word "aristocratic" denotes a broadmindedness bordering on recklessness. When, during the French Revolution, insurgents broke into the king's private chambers, Louis XVI, dullard though he was, burst into laughter, grabbed the Phrygian cap of one of the mob, put it casually on his own head, and shouted, "*Vive la France!*" Even those bloodthirsty revolutionaries were won over by the strange but perfectly natural dignity of his action, and in spite of themselves they yelled together with the king, "*Vive la France!*" and left his chambers meekly, without so much as lifting a finger against him. That's aristocracy: an artless, unstudied dignity. Primly closed mouths and well-adjusted collars one finds among the servants of the aristocracy. But for heaven's sake, don't call them "aristocratic"!

Because more or less all the people who were drinking beer with me on Kanran Hill that day appeared to be admirers of this author and asked me nothing but questions about him, I broke Bashō's rules and abused him, and as I abused him I grew more and more excited, until finally, eyebrows screwed up and mouth distorted, I ended with this strange digression on the meaning of "aristocratic." The others in the party did not show the least sign of agreement.

"Aristocratic!" muttered Mr. M. from Imabetsu, a perplexed look on his face. "None of us ever said such a silly thing!" He seemed annoyed by my drunken ranting. The others exchanged meaningful grins.

"In short . . ." I was almost shrieking. Ah, to hurl abuse at an older colleague is not something to be proud of. "Don't be fooled by a man's appearance. Louis XVI was one of the ugliest men in world history." I had lost my bearings completely.

"Anyway, I like his works," Mr. M. stated in a provocatively cut-and-dried tone.

"For Japan they're pretty good, aren't they?" Mr. H. from the hospital in Aomori said shyly, looking as if he wanted to mediate.

My position was becoming increasingly untenable.

"Perhaps . . . O.K., I'll grant you that. I suppose they are. But don't you people think it's a bit much to sit here without asking me a single thing about my own work?" And with a laugh I confessed what was really bothering me. Everyone smiled. Thinking that after all the best thing was to express my true feelings, I continued:

"My works are a muddle and a mess, but I cherish an ambition, and because that ambition is beyond my reach, you see me here reeling before you today. To you people I may seem slovenly, ignorant, and bedraggled, but I know what real class is. Dried confections shaped like pine needles, or a free-form arrangement of daffodils in a celadon vase—I don't think that has anything to do with class. Those are hobbies of the nouveaux riches—vulgar! Real class is a single white chrysanthemum on a great, pitch-black piece of rock. It has to be a big, filthy rock or it's no good. There is true class for you. You're still young, so you still believe that a carnation supported by wire and stuck in a vase is high-class art. Well, let me tell you: that's no more than the sham lyricism you find in a prep school for girls!"

This was strong language. "Do not blame the mote in the eyes of others, while ignoring the beam in your own." "It is exceedingly base to slander others but to praise oneself." The old poet's precepts contain a solemn truth. Indeed, it is exceedingly base. It is this base habit of mine that makes everybody in literary circles in Tokyo feel uncomfortable, and that makes them shun me as if I were a leper.

"It can't be helped." I was leaning backward, face to the sky, my back supported by my outstretched arms. "My work is absolutely terrible. I can't even begin to say how bad. Still, don't you think you could give it just one-tenth of the attention you're giving that beloved writer of yours? You don't look at my work at all, that's why I feel like spouting all this drivel. Take a look at it. Even one-twentieth will do. But look at it."

Everybody was in stitches. I felt much better for being laughed at. Mr. S., the head of the Kanita branch hospital, began to get to his feet.

"How about it? Shall we move the party elsewhere?" he asked in the benevolently soothing tones of the man of the world. At the E. Inn, the biggest in Kanita, a lunch had been prepared for everyone, he said. I looked inquiringly at T. to see if it was all right.

"Yes, why not? Let's accept the invitation." T. had got up and was putting his clothes back on. "We planned this in advance. Mr. S. says he's saved some top-grade *sake* from his rations, so why don't we all go and try some? We can't sponge off Mr. N. all the time."

I meekly fell in with T.'s proposal. That's why I feel reassured when he's around.

The E. Inn was not bad at all. The alcove in our room was arranged with taste, and the lavatory was clean, too. It struck me as a nice place to spend a night, even alone. On the whole the inns on the east coast of the Tsugaru Peninsula are superior to those on the west coast. I suppose it comes from having an ancient tradition of welcoming travelers from other provinces. In the old days the only way to cross to Hokkaido was to board a ship at Minmaya, so the Sotogahama Road was traveled night and day by people from all over the country. At the inn, too, we were served crab.

"I can see we're in Crab Paddy," someone said.

Because T. did not drink he had something to eat while the rest of us drank Mr. S.'s top-grade *sake*, postponing the meal until later. The more Mr. S. drank, the more cheerful he became.

"You see, I don't care whose novel it is, I like them all equally well. Once you start reading them, they're all interesting. Why, they've got to be pretty darn clever, these novelist types. That's why I can't help liking them. Name a novelist, and I like him, like him beyond reason. I have a little boy of three, you know, and I think I'll bring him up to be a novelist. His name is Fumio— that's written with the characters *fumi* for literature and *o* for man. His head is shaped a little like yours, if you don't mind my saying so. It looks like a pot without a lid: flat on top.''

This was the first time I had ever heard that my head looked like a pot without a lid. I trust I am perfectly aware of the various shortcomings of my appearance, but it had never struck me that even the shape of my head was peculiar. The discovery that I probably still had many defects I had never noticed, coming, as it did, immediately after I had abused a fellow author, made me feel frightfully uneasy. Mr. S. was getting merrier and merrier.

''Well, what do you think? We've just about finished the *sake*, so why don't you all come over to my house? Just for a little while. I'd like you to meet my wife and Fumio. Do, please. If you like cider, we've lots of it in Kanita. Come over and have some.''

He was doing his best to tempt me. It was very kind of him, but after the business about the shape of my head I was less than keen on going. I wanted to return quickly to N.'s place and take a nap. When I considered that at Mr. S.'s not just the top of my head but also its contents might be scrutinized, and that the results might turn out to be far from flattering, I was even less inclined to go. As usual, I looked to T. for advice. I was resolved that if T. said I should go, then that is what I would do.

T. looked serious as he considered the matter for a moment.

''I think you'd better go. Mr. S. is terribly drunk today, I know, but that's rare for him, and he *has* been looking forward to your visit for a long time.''

So I went. I decided not to worry too much about my head. On second thoughts I decided that Mr. S. must have been trying to be funny when he mentioned it. It doesn't help to brood over trifles like how one looks. More than good looks, what I lacked was self-confidence.

Though I'm from Tsugaru myself, I was a bit startled at our reception at Mr. S.'s, which in its frantic nature revealed the true character of the Tsugaru people. From the moment he entered, Mr. S. never once stopped bombarding his wife with orders.

"Hey, I've brought our guest from Tokyo! Finally I got him to come along! Here's that Dazai man we were talking about. Let me introduce him to you. Be a good woman and come over here quickly to pay your respects. And while you're at it, *sake*— or no, we already finished all the *sake*. Bring some cider. What, we only have one bottle? Not enough! Go buy two more, big ones! No, wait! Get one of those dried cod from the veranda and tear it up. No, wait, you've got to soften it first with a hammer or else you won't be able to tear it up properly. Stop! That's not the way to do it! Let me do it. To beat dried cod, you go like this, and this—ouch!—and this! Hey, soy sauce! We can't have cod without soy sauce. We're one, no, two cups short. Bring them quickly. No, wait, I guess those teacups will do. Well, cheers, cheers. Heeey! Go buy those bottles! No, wait, bring the kid. We'll have Dazai here see if he's got the makings of a novelist in him. What do you say, eh? This shape, isn't that what they call a pot without a lid? I really think it's like the shape of your head. Capital! Hey, take the kid away. He's a pain in the neck. It's vulgar to drag a dirty child like that in front of our guests! Isn't it? Typical nouveau riche! Quick, cider, four more liters, or our guests will escape. No, stop, you stay here and do the honors. Right, serve everyone. Go ask the old woman next door to go buy some cider for us. She wanted sugar, so give her some of ours. Wait, don't give it to her! Give all the sugar we have to our guest from Tokyo, to take home. All right? Don't forget now. Give it to him, all of it. Wrap it up in a newspaper, then in some oiled paper, tie a string around it, and give it to

53

him. Don't make the child cry! How vulgar! Typical nouveau riche! Wouldn't catch an aristocrat doing that. What are you up to now? Didn't I tell you the sugar was for when the guest leaves? Music, music! Put on a record. Schubert, Chopin, Bach, anything will do. Play some music. Stop! What's that? Bach? Turn it off. Can't hear yourself think with that noise! Put on something quieter. Wait, we've finished all the food. Fry up some angler-fish. We pride ourselves on the sauce in this house. Whether our guests will like it is another question, of course. Wait, give them fried anglerfish, and then *kayaki* of eggs in bean paste. You can only eat that in Tsugaru. Got it! Eggs in bean paste! Nothing like eggs in bean paste! Eggs in bean paste! Eggs in bean paste!''

There is not the slightest exaggeration in this account. This sort of tempestuous welcome is the Tsugaru way of showing affection.

Dried cod is cod (only big ones are used) that has been frozen and dried in a snowstorm. It has a refined, light taste that would have delighted the likes of Bashō. Mr. S. had five or six of them hanging from the beams of his veranda, and, staggering to his feet, he snatched off two or three, pounded them with in-discriminate hammerblows, hurt his left thumb, toppled over, and then crawled around on his knees to fill everyone's glass with cider. Now I understood that he hadn't been poking fun at me when he compared my head to a pot without a lid; he wasn't trying to be funny at all. Mr. S. apparently held a head of such shape in high regard. He seemed to think it a good thing. There is something touching in the simple honesty of Tsugaru people, something one must experience for oneself.

As for those cries of ''Eggs in bean paste! Eggs in bean paste!'' I think most of my readers will need some explanation. In Tsugaru, beef stew and chicken stew are called beef *kayaki* and chicken *kayaki*. I suppose in the dialect this is the pronunciation of *kai-yaki*, shell-fried. The custom appears to have died out, but when

I was a child the people here in Tsugaru used to cook meat in big scallop shells. They were convinced, it seems, that the shell created a broth. I wonder whether we did not perhaps inherit this custom from our Ainu predecessors. Be that as it may, we were all raised on *kayaki*. *Kayaki* of eggs in bean paste is a simple dish prepared in a clam shell: you sprinkle dried bonito shavings onto the bean paste, cook it, and then add an egg. In fact, it is really a dish for sick people. A sick person with a poor appetite is given this *kayaki* mixed with rice gruel. However, it is without doubt a typical Tsugaru dish, and it was this that prompted Mr. S. to shout out its name several times, determined that I should be treated to it. Almost on my knees I appealed to his wife that I had had quite enough, and so took my leave.

I would like the reader, however, to understand one thing. The welcome Mr. S. gave us that day is typical of the way Tsugaru people express affection. Real Tsugaru people are like that. And I know what I'm talking about—I often behave like Mr. S. Whenever I have friends visiting me from afar I am at a loss how to receive them. My heart pounding away, I run around in all directions but the right one, and I have even been known to hit my head against the lamp and knock over the shade. If guests show up unexpectedly while I am eating, I immediately throw my chopsticks aside and go to answer the door still chomping at my food, and I have been rewarded with many a good scowl for my efforts. But to keep a guest waiting while I serenely continue my repast is a feat I am not capable of. And like Mr. S., I am in essence deeply concerned about my guests' well-being. I offer them this and that and everything in the house trying to entertain them decently, but even so end up annoying them, with the result that I have to apologize afterward for my bad manners.

People from Tokyo, Osaka, and the other big cities probably think it rude and uncouth if you express your affection by forcing your guests at gunpoint to accept everything you own, including even your life, and they will most likely give you a wide berth for your pains. As I reflected on this, I felt Mr. S. had taught me something about myself, and on my way back home I couldn't help recalling him with fondness and pity. Visitors from other parts of the country will probably find the expressions of affection of Tsugaru people hard to swallow without—as it were—diluting them before consumption. Tokyo people give themselves airs and serve you food morsel by tiny morsel. I don't offer fresh mushrooms like Lord Kiso, but many is the time I have suffered the scorn of Tokyo's snooty socialites because of my excessive hospitality! For like Lord Kiso, I urge people, "Have some more! Do have some more!"[4]

I heard later that for one week afterward Mr. S. had to drown his embarrassment in *sake* whenever he recalled the eggs-in-bean-paste affair of that day. It seems he is usually twice as bashful and sensitive as other people. This is another characteristic of Tsugaru people. The true Tsugaru person is usually far from being a clumsy boor. He has a far more refined and delicate sense of understanding of others than the superficial city dweller. But when circumstances cause this pent-up feeling to burst through its dams and run out of control, he becomes quite flustered and cries in his confusion, to the utter disdain of the supercilious urbanite, "Eat these fresh mushrooms! Quick!"

The next day a friend visited Mr. S. as he sat drinking *sake*, still mortified, and asked him jokingly, "Well, did your wife give you an earful afterward?"

"No, not yet," answered Mr. S., as coy as a maiden.

He knew he had it coming.

1 (p. 43) *Thunder crackers.* So called because during the Edo period they were sold in front of the Kaminari, or Thunder, Gate in Asakusa, Tokyo.
2 (p. 47) *Blue flower.* In his unfinished novel *Heinrich von Ofterdingen,*

Novalis (Friedrich von Hardenberg, 1772–1801) uses the blue flower as a leitmotiv symbolizing man's infinite longing to fathom the true nature of love and beauty.

3 (p. 48) Dazai's criticisms in these paragraphs are leveled at Shiga Naoya (1883–1971), the much-admired author of a number of short stories and the autobiographical novel *A Dark Night's Passing* (*An'ya kōro*, 1937; trans. Edwin McClellan, 1976).

4 (p. 56) *Fresh mushrooms.* A reference to Book 8, Chapter 6, of the medieval epic *Heike monogatari* (*The Tale of the Heike*, trans. Hiroshi Kitagawa and Bruce Tsuchida, 1975). Minamoto no Yoshinaka (1154–84), a cousin of Yoritomo and Yoshitsune, had been brought up in the rural Kiso region and was not familiar with the finer points of etiquette as observed in the capital. He once offered plain, unsalted mushrooms to an imperial vice-councillor, but the refined nobleman was so horrified at Yoshinaka's display of rustic courtesy that he could hardly force himself to touch his food and finally fled in confusion.

III

Sotogahama

After leaving Mr. S.'s house we went back to N.'s place and drank some more beer. T. had been persuaded to spend the night, and the three of us slept in a room at the back of the house. But the next morning, while we were still asleep, T. took the bus back to Aomori. His work seemed to be keeping him pretty busy.

"Quite a cough he had, don't you think?" Although I had been asleep, my sharp ears had clearly picked up T.'s light, dry cough when he was getting dressed, and this filled me with a strange sadness. I mentioned it to N. as soon as I got up. N. was up, too, and was putting on his trousers.

"Yes, quite a cough," he said, a grave look on his face. When they are sober, drinkers usually wear a terribly grave look. And it's not just their faces; they really feel more serious in their hearts. "It wasn't a very healthy cough." Although he had appeared to be sleeping, N. had also heard it. "It's a matter of willpower." He sounded as if he wanted to dismiss the subject. He fastened his trouser belt. "Look at us. We got over it, didn't we?"

For a long time both N. and I had had to fight against respiratory diseases. N. used to suffer from severe asthma, but he seems to have conquered it completely now.

Before leaving on this journey, I had promised to send off a short story to a magazine published for our soldiers in Manchuria, and as the deadline was either that day or the next, I borrowed a quiet room for the whole of the following two days. Meanwhile, N. was working in one of the outbuildings of the rice refinery. On the evening of the second day he came to the room where I sat writing.

"Well, were you able to get a few pages down? I'll be through in about one more hour. I've finished a whole week's work in two days. If you know you're going to have a good time when you're through, your efficiency goes up like a shot. Just a little more. One last effort. . . ." He went back to the refinery, but within ten minutes he was in my room again.

"Well? Making any progress? *I'm* almost finished, you know. The machine's running beautifully these days. You haven't seen our mill yet, have you? It's a filthy place. Perhaps you'd better not. But I'll be in the mill if you need me." And back he went.

Then finally it filtered through my thick skull: he wanted to show me how valiantly he was toiling away in his refinery. He would be finished soon, so this was a hint to come and take a look before he was through. The realization brought a smile to my face. I quickly disposed of my story and went out to the refinery, which was in a separate building across the street. In patched-up corduroys, arms behind his back and an important look on his face, N. was standing next to a giant polishing machine that was rotating at a vertiginous speed.

"Pretty busy, eh?" I shouted.

N. turned around and smiled happily.

"Finished your work? Great! I'll be finished in a minute, too. Come in. Don't bother taking your clogs off."

But I'm not so inconsiderate as to enter a rice refinery with clogs on. N. himself had changed into immaculate straw sandals. No matter where I looked, however, there was nothing that resembled indoor slippers, so I just stood there at the door, grinning. I thought about going in barefoot, but then I realized that would seem exaggerated and hypocritical and would merely embarrass N., so I decided against it. It is one of my bad habits that I feel absurdly self-conscious when doing something perfectly acceptable.

"That's a pretty big machine, isn't it? Quite something to be able to handle it all by yourself!" I meant it. Like me, N. had never been very good at mechanics.

"No, it's simple. You turn the switch like this. . . ." And turning some switches here and there he demonstrated how the motor stopped dead, how he could produce a blizzard of chaff, how the finished rice came cascading down, in short, how he could operate the giant machine at will.

Suddenly my eye fell on a small poster stuck to a pillar in the center of the mill. A man with a head shaped like a *sake* flask, his legs crossed and his sleeves rolled up, was drinking *sake* out of a huge cup. The cup had a house and a barn drawn on it, and beneath it the legend "Don't drink up your health and your home." I stared at the poster for a long time, and I suppose N. noticed, for he looked at me and grinned broadly. I grinned, too. We were both guilty of the same offense. But what's a man to do, our grins asked. I sympathized with N. for having put up that poster. Who doesn't like to drink a few too many occasionally? In my case the cup should be decorated with my twenty-odd wretched publications—I have no house or barn I can drink up. And the legend should read "Don't drink up your health and your writings."

At the back of the mill two large machines were standing idle. I asked N. what they were.

"Those?" he answered with a faint sigh. "One is for making ropes and the other a loom for weaving straw mats, but I can't handle them: they're rather difficult to operate. Some four or five years ago we had a terrible harvest, and all of a sudden there was no work for the refinery. Day after day I sat worrying by the hearth, puffing at cigarettes and searching for a way out, until finally I bought these two machines, put them in a corner of the mill, and tried to see if I could work them. But I'm clumsy, and somehow I just couldn't manage. Those were bad times. Six people in the house, and none of them working! I really wondered what was to become of us."

N. has one child, a four-year-old boy, but he has also taken in the three children of his younger sister and her husband, both of whom are dead (N.'s brother-in-law was killed while fighting at the front in northern China). N. and his wife are bringing up the three orphans as if it were the most normal thing in the world, loving them just as much as their own child. According to his wife, N. even tends to spoil them.

One of the three, the eldest boy, is a student at Aomori Technical School. One Saturday, instead of taking the bus, he walked all the way—more than thirty kilometers—from Aomori to his home in Kanita, where he arrived about midnight. He knocked on the door and shouted, "Uncle! Uncle!" N. flew out of bed, opened the door, and hugged the boy ecstatically. "You walked all the way? Really? You walked?" That was all he could say, but then he let fly at his wife and fired off one order after another. "Give him some hot water and sugar. Fry some rice cakes for him. Warm up some noodles." When his wife began to protest that the child was tired and wanted to go to sleep, he shouted, "What? Whaaaat?" and shook his fist at her in an utterly exaggerated manner. This was altogether too preposterous a quarrel. Their nephew burst into laughter, N.—fist still in the air—followed suit, his wife began to laugh too, and they were quickly reconciled. This episode reveals admirably what sort of person N. is.

"Well, life has its ups and downs. There's always something," I said. But when I compared my own life with his, I was suddenly moved to tears. I could clearly imagine the sad figure of this good man, my friend, trying to weave straw mats on the loom with his unwilling hands, alone in a corner of his mill. I love this friend.

That night we used the fact that we had both finished our jobs as an excuse to sit down together for a few beers. We discussed the question of harvest failures in our native region. N. belongs to the Society for the Study of the History of Aomori Prefecture, so he has quite a lot of literature on the subject.

"Look at this," he said, opening a book. The pages he showed me contained the following table, a miserable record of the harvest failures in Tsugaru:

1615 Disaster	1707 Disaster	1833 Disaster
1616 "	1716 Failure	1835 "
1640 "	1720 "	1836 "
1641 "	1737 "	1837 Failure
1642 Failure	1740 "	1838 Disaster
1656 "	1745 Disaster	1839 Failure
1666 "	1747 Failure	1866 "
1671 "	1749 Disaster	1869 "
1674 "	1755 "	1873 "
1675 "	1767 Failure	1889 "
1679 "	1776 Poor	1891 "
1681 Disaster	1782 Disaster	1897 "
1684 Failure	1783 "	1902 Disaster
1692 Disaster	1786 "	1905 "
1694 "	1787 Poor	1913 Failure
1695 "	1789 Failure	1931 "
1696 Failure	1793 "	1934 "
1702 Poor	1799 "	1935 "
1705 Failure	1813 "	1940 Poor
1706 "	1832 Poor	

One does not have to be born in Tsugaru to be moved when

reading this table. Between the summer of 1615, when the forces of Toyotomi Hideyori were destroyed at the siege of Osaka Castle, and the present day, a timespan of some 350 years, the harvest failed about sixty times. That means a harvest failure almost every five years.

N. showed me another book:

The next year, 1833, an east wind raged incessantly from the first day of spring, an auspicious day, to the Doll Festival on the third day of the third month, so the drifts of snow would not melt and the farmers had to use sledges to carry the snow off their fields. By the fifth month the seedlings were still very small, but the shortness of the growing season made further postponement impossible and they were planted out as they were. The easterly winds blew stronger every day, and in the sixth month, midsummer, a canopy of dense clouds covered the heavens, and so gloomy did the weather become that a view of the sun and the blue sky became a great rarity. . . .

Morning and evening all that midsummer month it was so cold that people had to wear their padded winter clothes. The nights were especially cold. It was now the seventh month, the time of year when the Nebuta festival is held. [This is an annual Tsugaru festival, held around the seventh day of the seventh month of the lunar calendar. Young people, dressed up in all sorts of costumes, dance through the streets in a parade pulling huge lanterns, which are shaped like warriors, dragons, or tigers painted in brilliant colors, and mounted on wagons. Part of the excitement always consists in bumping into the lanterns made by other neighborhoods and fighting it out. Tradition has it that Sakanoue no Tamuramaro used this kind of lantern on his expedition against the Ezo to lure the barbarians out of their mountains before massacring them, though such explanations are largely apocryphal. Similar parades are held not only in Tsugaru but all over the northeast, so the Nebuta lanterns should probably be considered a local variation of the floats used in the other summer festivals of the north, and not so different from those of Tokyo's summer festival.] However, not a mosquito raised its voice along the roads; indoors they made but the faintest of sounds—it was not even necessary to use mosquito nets. The chirping of the cicada had become rare indeed.

About the sixth day of the seventh month it grew hot, and in the days before the Festival of the Dead people put on their summer clothes. From about the thirteenth, ears began to appear on most of the early rice. The people were elated and performed the festival dances with great enthusiasm. But on the fifteenth and sixteenth the sun gradually assumed the dull sheen of a midnight mirror, and on the night of the seventeenth—just before dawn, when most of the dancers and revelers had gone home—there was an unexpected and severe frost. The tender ears hung their heads, and young and old lamented loud and long at the sight.[1]

A cry of dismay is about the only comment one can make about such conditions. When we were children, the old people often told us about the misery and wretchedness of the *kegazu* (in Tsugaru, a disastrous harvest is called *kegazu*, perhaps deriving from the standard *kikatsu*, starvation), and we toddlers would be so affected by their gloomy stories that we invariably burst into tears. Back in my homeland after all these years and confronted with such records, I felt an instinctive indignation that went beyond mere sorrow.

"This is too much!" I said. "They tell us all those beautiful stories about how this is the age of science, and they can't even teach the farmers how to prevent such bad harvests. They're a useless lot!"

"But the agronomists are doing all sorts of research. They've come up with improved varieties that are more resistant to the cold and with new planting techniques, so we no longer have complete harvest failures as we did in the past. But still, you know, despite all that, we have a bad time of it every five years or so."

"A useless lot!" I spat out, my anger directed at no one in particular.

N. laughed.

"Other people have to live in the middle of the desert. Getting angry doesn't help, you know. And this climate also produces a unique capacity for kindness."

"Some kindness! Bungling and boorish! No wonder I always feel overwhelmed by artists from the south."

"But you don't give in to them, do you? In all its history, Tsugaru has never been defeated by invaders. Hurt, yes, but beaten, never! Why else would they call the Eighth Division a national treasure?"[2]

We members of the present generation are, after all, of the same blood as our ancestors, who had to fight famine as soon as they were born and were nursed on nothing but rain and the raw elements. Of course I would prefer to be graceful and elegant instead of bungling and boorish, but I am stuck with my ancestors' blood and can do no more than work like a horse to nurture my talents. I have no choice in the matter. Perhaps it is better not to sigh over the sorrows of the past, but, like N., to take pride in this tradition of toil and hardship as if it were our princely birthright. Besides, those scenes of infernal misery will not repeat themselves forever, not even in Tsugaru.

The next day, with N. as my guide, I took the bus up the Sotogahama Road to spend a night in Minmaya and then walk on up the desolate road along the shore to Cape Tappi, the northernmost tip of Honshu. In each of the bleak and windswept hamlets between Minmaya and Tappi the robustness of the Tsugaru people is touchingly apparent: defiant before gales and unyielding before the violence of waves, they struggle to feed their families. In the villages south of Minmaya, especially in Minmaya itself and in Imabetsu, I could see how serene life can be in the cheerful atmosphere of those trim, well-appointed harbors. Ah, let us cast aside our fears of famine!

The following felicitous passage is by the scientist Satō Hiroshi. I will borrow it to disperse my readers' gloom, and also as a toast to a bright new start for us Tsugaru people. Professor Satō writes in his *Introduction to the Industries of Ōshū*:

Ōshū—domain of the Ezo, so swift to take cover at every attack and so swift to retreat into their mountains when pursued. Ōshū—where everywhere the massive mountain ranges form a natural barrier to human traffic. Ōshū—surrounded by the Japan Sea, tempestuous and inhospitable, and the Pacific Ocean, its waters barred in their course by the jagged Kamikita Mountains. Ōshū—with its thick winter mantle of snow, coldest place in all of Honshu, since time immemorial plagued by failed harvests. Pitiful Ōshū—with barely fifteen percent of its land arable, compared to twenty-five percent in Kyushu. Thus handicapped in every respect by unfavorable natural conditions, how can Ōshū manage, on what industries does Ōshū rely, to feed its 6.3 million people?

The geography books all tell us that Ōshū lies in Honshu's farthest northeastern corner, and that food, clothing, and shelter there are all of a rudimentary kind. In the past the roofs were thatched with grass, shingles, or cedar bark, but nowadays most people live under tin-plate roofs. They cover their heads with kerchiefs, wear baggy working pants, and from the middle classes down content themselves with very plain fare. Is this really true? Does the land of Ōshū have so little in the way of industry? Is the north the only part of the country yet to be touched by the twentieth century, a century so proud of its great speed?

No, that is already an Ōshū of the past. Before one can discuss the Ōshū of today, one should recognize that it is imbued with the same pent-up energy that existed in Italy immediately before the Renaissance. Culture and industry have benefited from Emperor Meiji's interest in education, which rapidly made its influence felt even in Ōshū's remotest nooks and corners. The harsh nasal twang so characteristic of the speech of its people disappears as the standard language is promoted. The dwelling place of ignorant, barbarian tribes which once wallowed in the mire of primitive conditions has received the bright light of education, and behold! Reclamation follows reclamation, and day by day the number of fertile fields increases. Improvement follows improvement, and every day the cattle, forestry, and fishing industries wax richer. What bodes even better is that with its low population density the region has a high potential for future development.

Like the swarms of migratory birds—the starlings, ducks, tits, and geese—that roam this region in search of food, the Japanese people moved north toward Ōshū from all over the country during the period of the expansion of the Yamato state, and while they were subjugating the Ezo they roamed east and west, lured by the natural resources, the game in the mountains, or the fish in the streams. Thus, after several generations, the people had put down roots wherever they chose, and were growing rice in the plains of Akita, Shōnai, and Tsugaru, or experimenting with afforestation in the mountains of the north, raising horses on the moors, or fishing along the coast. They laid the basis for the prosperous industries of today. The 6.3 million people of the six prefectures of Ōshū do not neglect the distinctive industries of their ancestors, but increasingly they seek new ways to develop them. The migratory birds may roam forever, but the rough-and-ready people of the north need wander no more: they grow their rice, sell their apples, run their splendid glossy-coated colts on the wide moors that border the majestic forests, and steer into harbor boats filled to the gunwales with their dancing, silvery catch.

I feel so utterly gratified by this encomium that I almost want to run up to the author and shake him by the hand.

That day N. was going to guide me up the Ōshū Sotogahama coast, but before we could leave we first had to solve a certain problem.

"What will you take with you to drink? Shall I put a few bottles of beer in your rucksack?"

Mrs. N.'s question cut me to the quick. I wondered why I was born a member of that disreputable tribe known as drinkers.

"No, please don't worry. I can do without. It's all right. Really," I sputtered in confusion as I hoisted my rucksack onto my back and fled from the house.

"You know, every time I hear the word 'drink,' " I explained to N., who had followed me out, "it gives me a jolt and makes me feel as if I'm sitting on a bed of thorns."

N. appeared to agree with me and chuckled, his face red: "Me, now, when I'm alone I've no problems, but with you around I can't do without a drink. By the way, Mr. M. of Imabetsu was saying he'd ask his neighbors for some of their *sake* rations and keep it for us, so let's stop by his place."

I sighed ambiguously. "I'm causing everyone a lot of trouble."

We had intended to go directly from Kanita to Tappi by boat and then come back on foot and by bus, but that day such a strong easterly wind had been blowing since early in the morning that the weather had earned itself the designation "stormy" and the boat we had planned to take had been canceled. We changed our plans accordingly and left by bus instead. Surprisingly enough, the bus was empty, and both of us had ample room to sit comfortably. After we had driven north along the Sotogahama Road for about an hour, the wind gradually died down, the clouds parted, and it began to seem as if the ferries would be sailing according to schedule after all. We decided that we would first stop at Mr. M.'s in Imabetsu, and if it looked as if the ships were sailing, we would relieve him of some of his *sake* and go straight to Imabetsu harbor. To take the same overland route there and back seemed stupid and uninteresting. N. pointed out the various sites from the bus windows and explained them to me, but by and by we had approached a zone of strategic importance, so I must be careful not to record his explanations in too much detail. Anyway, we saw no trace of the dwellings of the old Ezo, but every village looked snug and cheerful, perhaps because the weather had cleared up.

The famous Kyoto doctor Tachibana Nankei wrote in his *Records of a Journey to the East*, which was published in the last decade of the eighteenth century:

> Never since the dawn of history has the nation known such peace as now. From Yaku Island in the Kikai Archipelago in the west to Sotogahama in Ōshū in the east, there is not a place that does not observe the law. In the past, Yaku sounded almost like the name of some foreign country, and until fairly recently Ōshū was still partly inhabited by the Ezo, as can be seen from many place names in Tsugaru and Nanbu. The villages of Sotogahama have names like Tappi, Horozuki, Uchimappe, Sotomappe, Imabetsu, and Utetsu. These are all Ezo names. Even nowadays the customs of the

villagers from Utetsu and thereabouts resemble somewhat those of the Ezo, and the Tsugaru people despise the inhabitants of that village, saying they are of barbarous origin.[3] However, to my mind not only the people from around Utetsu, but most of the country people of Tsugaru and Nanbu are of Ezo ancestry. Only in places that basked early in the warmth of the emperor's rule did the people change their language and customs sufficiently to appear to be of Japanese ancestry. Hence it is only natural that a refined culture has not yet developed here.

Some 150 years have passed since Nankei wrote these lines, and if we could call him back to life, put him on a bus, and make him travel this smooth concrete road, he would twist and crane his neck in mute amazement. Or would he? Perhaps he would sigh for the "snows of yesteryear."

Nankei's chronicles of his travels are, it seems, counted among the famous books of the Edo period, but their author himself acknowledges in his Introduction:

I undertook these journeys for the sake of medical science and took care to record even the most insignificant pieces of medical information for the benefit of my colleagues, but I also jotted down all sorts of things that I saw and heard on the road, though I have not been able to verify their authenticity and must therefore assume that this book is full of errors.

In other words, he records one tall tale after another, satisfied merely to tickle his readers' curiosity. I will not mention what he says of other regions but will restrict my examples to what he writes about Sotogahama. He tells us without the slightest qualification:

The port where one embarks to cross from Sotogahama in the Tsugaru domain to Matsumae is Minmaya in Ōshū, in the extreme northeast of the country. [Minmaya was written with different characters in those days.] After his escape from Takadate, Minamoto no Yoshitsune had come this far and was about to cross to Ezo when he was delayed here for several days by unfavorable winds. Because of the urgency of the situation, he placed a statue of Kannon that he was carrying with him on top of a rock in the sea and prayed for a fair wind. Instantly the wind changed direction, and he was able to cross to Matsumae without mishap. That statue is now in a temple here and is known as the Kannon to Which Yoshitsune Prayed for Wind. There is, in addition, on the shore near Minmaya, a huge rock with three holes, one next to the other, like stables. Here Yoshitsune's horses were given shelter, and thus the place is known as Minmaya, Three-Horse Stable.

Elsewhere he writes:

In Tsugaru's Sotogahama, in Ōshū, there is a place called Tairadate, to the north of which a rocky promontory juts out into the sea. It is known as Ishizaki-no-Hana, Cape Stone-Nose. A little further on is Shudani, the Vermilion Valley, where from between soaring mountains a slender brook flows out into the sea. All the stones and rocks in this valley are vermilion in color. The very water is red, and the wet rocks look startlingly brilliant with their colors glistening in the morning sun. Even the pebbles in the sea near the mouth of the brook are mostly vermilion, and it is said that the fish in the sea here are all red, too. It is wondrous how sentient and insentient creatures, fish and stones alike, have all been turned a vermilion hue by the cinnabar lode in this valley.

And when you think he is done, he startles you even more with an account of a strange fish that lives in the northern seas and goes by the name of Old Man:

It is some two or three leagues long, and no one has ever seen all of its body. When it makes one of its rare appearances on the surface, it seems to the human eye as if a number of large islands are rising out of the sea, but these are only a part of its back and fins. It swallows whales some sixty to seventy feet long like a whale swallows sardines, and so whales scatter in all directions when this fish appears.

And elsewhere:

One night in Minmaya, some old people who lived in the neighborhood came to the house where I was staying and joined the family's grandparents. They sat around the sunken hearth and told one another all sorts of stories.

"The most horrible thing that happened to us in the last twenty or thirty years was the Matsumae tidal wave. There was not a breath of wind and no sign of rain, but for some reason the sky clouded over, and at night wherever you looked shining objects streaked across the heavens. Finally, four or five days before the disaster—and this was really terrifying—we saw gods flying through the sky, even in broad daylight. Some were mounted on horseback in their ancient clothes, others were riding dragons or clouds, still others were seated on rhinoceroses or elephants; some were dressed in white, others in red and green; some were big, others small. Buddhas and gods of all sorts and appearances flew through the sky in all directions. Everyone went outside and every day we offered prayers, observing and discussing these miraculous events for four or five days. Then, one evening, as we were looking out over the sea, an object appeared in the distance which looked like a mountain of the purest snow. 'Look over there! Now something strange has come out of the sea!' As we were speaking, it gradually drew closer, and then we saw that it was a huge wave, higher than the top of the mountain on that island over there. 'A tidal wave! Quick! Run!' Old and young, men and women, scrambled for their lives, but rapidly the wave drew nearer and swept everything out to the bottom of the sea: people, houses, paddies, fields, plants, trees, even birds and animals. Nothing was left. In the villages along the coast not a soul survived. Overawed, we said to one another that assuredly the gods must have flown through the sky to let us know something terrible was going to happen here and to warn us that we must leave this place.''

All these miraculous and dreamlike happenings are rendered in a matter-of-fact but fluent style.

In the present circumstances it does not seem advisable to give too detailed a description of the scenery in this part of Sotogahama. Instead, for all their absurdities, I thought it might be fun to copy parts of this old travelogue and become immersed in its fairy-tale atmosphere. I had originally copied down a few more excerpts from *Records of a Journey to the East*, but I will limit myself to only one, a passage that seems to me likely to be of special interest to people who are fond of literature:

During my stay in Tsugaru's Sotogahama, in Ōshū, the local magistrate was scouring the land for people from Tango. When I asked why, I was told that the goddess of Tsugaru's Mount Iwaki detests Tango people. The weather would turn foul with incessant wind and rain, ships would be unable to set sail, and the Tsugaru domain would be afflicted with terrible hardships, were someone from Tango to enter the region, even in secret. Because a tempest had been raging since my arrival, the authorities were checking to see whether someone from Tango had entered the domain. Whenever the weather turns bad, the magistrate issues stern orders that anyone from Tango should be expelled immediately. As soon as the offender has left the Tsugaru domain, the weather clears up and the wind dies down. It is remarkable how not only the common people entertain this traditional hatred, but how even the authorities launch an investigation on every such occasion. This hatred of Tango people is strongest in Aomori, Minmaya, and the other ports of Sotogahama.

This was all very mysterious. I tried to get a precise answer to my question and was told that it stemmed from the goddess of Mount Iwaki being the incarnation of the Lady Anju, who was born in these parts. The Lady Anju was maltreated by Sanshō the Steward during her wanderings in the land of Tango, and ever since the goddess of Mount Iwaki in her anger summons forth wind and rain and storms whenever someone from that region visits Tsugaru.

Because almost everybody along the ninety-league length of the Sotogahama coast depends for his living on fishing or shipping, they are always hoping for the fairest of winds. Consequently, when the weather takes a turn for the worse, the whole region curses the people of Tango. The same thing happens in the ports of neighboring domains such as Matsumae and Nanbu, where people from Tango are often so hated that they are turned away. How deep run the currents of human resentment!

A strange story, and pretty annoying for the people of Tango (the northern part of modern Kyoto Prefecture). If anyone from Tango visited Tsugaru in those days, he was asking for certain trouble.

As children we learned the story of Anju and Zushiō from picture books, and anyone at all interested in fiction will know it from Mori Ōgai's masterpiece ''Sanshō the Steward.''[4]

However, very few people seem to have heard that the beautiful brother and sister of this sad story were born in Tsugaru and deified on Mount Iwaki after their death. In fact, I myself have my reservations. The story comes from Nankei, who wrote without batting an eyelid that Yoshitsune escaped to Tsugaru, that there are fish two leagues long, and that red rocks can dye the water of a river and the scales of fish, so this too perhaps is one of those unreliable reports of which Nankei says he has been unable to verify the authenticity. To be sure, the tradition that Anju and Zushiō were from Tsugaru is also mentioned in the *Illustrated Encyclopedia of Japan and China*, in the entry on "The Avatars of Mount Iwaki." Because its language is so archaic, it is rather difficult to read, but what it says is this:

> According to legend, one of the ancient lords of this region [Tsugaru] was called Iwaki Hangan Masa'uji. While he was staying in Kyoto in the winter of the first year of Eihō [1081], he was slandered and banished to Kyushu. He had left behind him in his home in the country his two children. The eldest, a daughter, was called Anju; the son, Zushiō. In their search for their father, the children and their mother crossed all of Dewa and finally wandered as far as Naoe Bay in Echigo.

So far the account is fairly clear, but at the end it grows ambiguous:

> It is strange that they should be deified on Mount Iwaki in Tsugaru, more than a hundred leagues to the north of Iwaki Province.

In Ōgai's "Sanshō the Steward," they leave "their home in Shinobugōri in Iwashiro." I think the confusion caused by the fact that the characters for Iwashiro can be misread as Iwaki may well have been responsible for this legend ending up on Mount Iwaki.[5] Be that as it may, the old Tsugaru people used to believe firmly that Anju and Zushiō were Tsugaru children, and that the detestable steward was so accursed that the weather in Tsugaru turned bad whenever someone from Tango entered the region. To those of us who sympathize with Anju and Zushiō, that thought is not without its charm.

Here let us leave the legends of Sotogahama. At about noon our bus arrived in Imabetsu, where Mr. M. lives. As I have said before, Imabetsu is a cheerful—one would almost like to say modern—port. Its population is perhaps close to four thousand. N. took me to Mr. M.'s house, but when we called, Mrs. M. came out and told us her husband was not at home. She seemed to be a little out of sorts. When I see members of a family in this frame of mind, I always wonder whether they aren't perhaps quarreling about me. Sometimes I'm right, and sometimes I'm wrong. The appearance of a writer or journalist tends to be a cause for concern in a law-abiding household. For us writers too it is a painful experience, and any writer who has never known this feeling must be a fool indeed.

"Where did he go?" N. was not at all put out. He took off his backpack. "We'll rest here for a moment if you don't mind." And he sat down on the doorstep.

"I'll go and call him."

"That's very good of you." N. is a model of imperturbability. "Is he at the hospital?"

"Yes, I think so," the attractive but shy Mrs. M. said softly as she slipped on her clogs and went out. Her husband works in a hospital in Imabetsu.

I sat down on the doorstep next to N., and together we waited for Mr. M.

"Did you tell him we were coming?"

"Well, sort of." N. was calmly puffing at a cigarette.

"We shouldn't have arrived just at lunchtime." I was a little worried.

"Yes, but we've brought our own lunch." He was quite unconcerned. This, I thought, was the sort of man Saigō Takamori must have been.

Mr. M. showed up.

"Do come in," he said, with self-conscious joviality.

"No, I'm afraid we can't." N. stood up. "If the ships are sailing, we'd like to board the ferry for Tappi right away."

"I see," Mr. M. nodded lightly. "Then I'll go and find out whether they are or not."

He went all the way to the pier to ask, but it turned out that services were still suspended.

"It can't be helped." My trusty guide showed not the least sign of despondency. "In that case, do you mind if we rest here for a while and eat our lunch?"

"Yes, here on the doorstep is fine." My display of deference knew no bounds.

"But won't you come in?" Mr. M. asked timidly.

"Why not." Calmly, N. began to untie his puttees. "Let's have a nice long think about the next leg of our trip."

We were shown into our host's study. A red-hot charcoal fire lay crackling in a small sunken hearth. The shelves were chock-full of books, including the collected works of Valéry and Izumi Kyōka. I suppose Nankei, who concluded with such confidence that "it is only natural that a refined culture has not yet developed here," would be dumbfounded by the scene in this room.

"We've got *sake* in the house," said the courteous Mr. M., taking it on himself to blush on our behalf. "Shall we have a drink?"

"No, no, if we drink here . . . ," N. began, suppressing a chuckle.

"That's all right." Our host had guessed our problem. "It's not the *sake* you're taking to Tappi. I've put that aside, so . . ."

"Hoho!" N. whooped. "No, really! If we drink something now, we'll never make it to Tappi today."

While N. was going on in this vein, Mrs. M. silently brought in some flasks of *sake*. I changed my mind about her to our advantage, and decided that perhaps she was naturally silent and not especially angry with us.

"Well then, shall we have just a little and try not to get drunk?" I suggested to N.

"If we drink, we'll get drunk," N. declared in the tones of one who is older and wiser. "Perhaps we'd better spend tonight in Minmaya."

"That's a good idea. For today, just have a good time here. The walk to Minmaya takes—oh—no more than an hour or so, I guess, even if you dawdle all the way. No matter how drunk you are, you can easily make it." Such was Mr. M.'s advice. Having decided to spend the night in Minmaya, we began to drink.

Ever since I had entered the room, one thing had been bothering me: sitting there on Mr. M.'s desk was a collection of essays by the author I had so casually vilified in Kanita. Faithful readers deserve our respect. I could see that no matter how much I had slandered and abused that writer on Kanran Hill, it had not had the least effect on Mr. M.'s opinion of him.

"Excuse me, but could I take a look at that?" As it simply wouldn't leave me in peace, I finally asked Mr. M. for the book, flipped it open, and began to read with an eagle eye. I had really been hoping to find some flaw and then crow over my victory, but the passage I read appeared to be one the author had written with special care: I found not a blemish in it. Silently I read on. One page, two pages, three pages. Finally I had read five pages, and put the book away.

"The passage I've just read has something to be said for it, but his other writings are full of weak spots," I said, unwilling to admit defeat.

Mr. M. seemed pleased.

"It's because the book looks so gorgeous," I muttered, still loath to admit I was beaten. "On this kind of first-class paper and printed in such big type, almost anything looks good."

Mr. M., instead of accepting the challenge, just sat there smiling. It was a victor's smile. However, in my heart I didn't really mind. I had read a decent piece of writing and felt relieved. How much better that is than to find fault and wallow in triumph! I'm not lying. I love good literature.

In Imabetsu there is a temple called Hongakuji, famous for having once had the great Teiden as its chief priest. Takeuchi Unpei mentions him in his *History of Aomori Prefecture*:

> The priest Teiden was born the son of Niiyama Jinzaemon of Imabetsu. At an early age he became a novice at Seiganji in Hirosaki, after which he studied for fifteen years at Senshōji in Iwakidaira. At the age of twenty-nine he became chief priest of Hongakuji in Imabetsu, where he lived until his death, at the age of forty-two, in 1731. The influence of his teaching was not limited to Tsugaru, but extended to adjacent provinces. In 1727, for instance, the solemn consecration of a gilt-bronze stupa drew throngs of pious men and women, from Tsugaru of course, but also from Nanbu, Akita, and Matsumae.

"Shall we take a look at the temple?" said my guide to Sotogahama, town councillor N. "Literary discussions are all very well, but those ideas of yours are not for popular consumption. They're weird, and that's why you'll never become famous, no matter how long you wait. Take the priest Teiden now. . . ." N. was pretty drunk. "Take the priest Teiden now. He didn't begin by preaching Buddhism, he tried to improve the quality of the people's lives first. You have to do that, or people won't listen to the teachings of Buddha or anyone else. Why, Teiden promoted industry, he . . ." At this point N. burst into laughter. "Anyway, let's go and have a look. You can't come all the way to Imabetsu and then not see Hongakuji. Teiden is the pride of Sotogahama. But here I am saying all this, and I've never been to see the temple either. This is a good chance—I want to see it today. Come on, let's all go together.''

I had wanted to stay where we were and, over a few flasks of *sake*, discuss my ''weird literary ideas'' with Mr. M., who appeared to be similarly inclined. However, N. seemed really steamed up about Teiden, and he finally got us off our lazy behinds.

''Fine. We'll stop by at Hongakuji and then walk straight on to Minmaya.'' I sat down on the doorstep and, tying on my puttees, turned to Mr. M. ''How about it? Won't you join us?''

''Yes, I'll gladly keep you company as far as Minmaya.''

''That's great, thanks. In fact, I was a little afraid that in his present state the town councillor might regale me with a long speech on Kanita politics in our Minmaya lodgings tonight. If you're with us, I'll feel safer. Mrs. M., we're borrowing your husband tonight.''

''Oh,'' and a smile was the only reply. She seemed fairly used to it, or perhaps it was more a case of her being resigned to all eventualities.

Having had our water containers filled with *sake*, we started out in good cheer. On the way, N. droned on and on about Teiden this and Teiden that. The roof of the temple had already come into sight when we met an old woman selling fish. The cart she was pulling was full and there was a great variety. I spotted a sea bream over half a meter long.

''How much is that bream?'' I asked, because I had absolutely no idea of the price of fish outside of Tokyo.

''One yen seventy.''

Cheap, I thought. I ended up buying it, but once I had bought it I didn't know what to do with it. We were on our way to a temple. Visiting a temple with half a meter of fish under one's arm is an unusual practice. I was at a loss.

"That was a stupid thing to go and buy." N. curled the corners of his mouth in scorn. "What on earth are you going to do with it?"

"Well, I was thinking of taking it to our lodgings in Minmaya to have the whole thing broiled in one piece and served on a big dish so that the three of us could nibble at it."

"You do have some weird ideas. Now we look as if we're on our way to a wedding."[6]

"Still, don't you think it's nice to be able to have a taste of luxury for just one yen seventy?"

"Not in the least! One yen seventy is a lot around here. That was a lousy bargain you drove."

"I guess so." I was crestfallen.

Finally we entered the temple grounds, with me still lugging that big bream.

"What shall I do?" I whispered to Mr. M. "This has got me stumped."

"Yes, I see." Mr. M. gave the matter serious thought. "I'll go to the temple and ask for a newspaper or something. Just wait here for a moment, will you?"

He went off to the priest's quarters and after a little while returned with a newspaper and a piece of string. He wrapped up the problem bream and put it in my rucksack for me. That load off my mind, I looked at the main gate of the temple, but saw nothing particularly splendid about it.

"Nothing special about this temple, is there?" I whispered to N.

"No, no, no! The interior is better than the outside. Anyway, let's go in and listen to what the priest has to say."

I was not enthusiastic. I followed N. only reluctantly, and in this case my instinct proved correct for we did, in fact, come to grief. The temple priest was not at home, but a woman in her fifties—his wife, I suppose—came out and took us to the main hall, where she began a long, long explanation. We were obliged to kneel down and sit on our heels and listen respectfully. Finally the lecture seemed to have come to an end and I was just about to get up, glad the ordeal was over, when N. shuffled forward on his knees.

"I have a question, if you don't mind," he said. "I wonder when the priest Teiden built this temple."

"I beg your pardon? Saint Teiden did not build this temple, he restored its spiritual authority. He was the temple's fifth priest. . . ." And yet another long explanation followed.

"Is that so?" N. looked dazed. "Well, then I have one more question: this priest Teizan. . . ." He actually said Teizan! He had lost his grip altogether.

Edging further and further forward in his excitement, N. continued his question-and-answer game, until finally only a hair's breadth separated his knees from those of the old woman. It had begun to get dark, and I was beginning to worry about whether we would still be able to make it to Minmaya.

"The calligraphy on that big tablet over there is the work of Ōno Kurōbei."

"Really?" N. was struck with admiration. "By Ōno Kurōbei you mean . . ."

"I expect you've heard of him, one of the forty-seven samurai." At least, that's what I think she said.[7] "That gentleman died in these parts, at the age of forty-two. They say that he was a very religious person who from time to time donated large sums of money to this temple."

At this moment Mr. M. finally got to his feet, walked up to the old woman, reached into his inner pocket and gave her some money wrapped in white paper, bowed politely without a word, then turned toward N. and said softly, "It's time we took our leave."

"What? Oh. Yes, let's go," N. said benignly. "That was an

extremely interesting talk," he complimented the old lady, and at long last got to his feet. When we asked him later, he said he could not remember a single word of what she had said. We were aghast.

"But you looked so interested when you asked all those questions!"

"Oh, I wasn't paying attention at all. Why, I was drunk as a lord! I thought you were the ones who wanted to know these things, so I put up with it and asked the old woman some questions. I sacrificed myself!" Some sacrifice!

When we arrived at our lodgings in Minmaya, the sun had already set. We were shown to a comfortable little room on the second floor, at the front. The inns of Sotogahama all seem to be too good for their towns. Our room looked out over the sea. It had begun to drizzle, and the sea was white and calm.

"Not bad, eh? We can have the bream and a nice, long drink while we watch the rain fall on the sea." I pulled the wrapped-up fish out of my rucksack and gave it to the maid. "This is a sea bream. Broil it as it is, please, and then bring it back here."

The maid did not look very bright. "Oh," was all she could say. She accepted the package with a blank look and left the room.

"Did she understand?" Like me, N. seemed to have his misgivings about the maid. He called her back and explained once more. "Broil it as it is. There are three of us, but that doesn't mean you have to cut it into three pieces. Remember! There's no need to divide it into three equal portions. Do you understand?" N.'s explanation was not as clear as it might have been. The maid's reply—another "Oh"—did not sound encouraging.

Presently the trays were brought up. "They're broiling the bream, but there's no *sake* today," our less-than-brilliant maid announced woodenly.

"Can't be helped. We'll drink the *sake* we brought."

"What else can we do?" said N., and in no time he had produced the containers. "Could you bring up two flasks and three cups?"

While we were still joking to each other that in this case it had not been necessary to specify the exact number, the bream was served. N.'s instructions that it did not have to be cut into three identically sized pieces had produced an idiotic result: on an ordinary, off-white dish lay—without head, tail, or bones— five slices of broiled bream.

I am not in the least fussy about food. I expect my readers will understand that I hadn't bought such a big bream just because I wanted to eat it. I had wanted to admire it as it lay served on a big dish, broiled in its original shape. To eat, or not to eat, was not the question. I had wanted to feel that glow of luxury, sipping my *sake* and looking at the fish. N.'s way of putting it— "that doesn't mean you have to cut it into three pieces"—had been strange, but I felt like stamping on the floor out of anger at the exasperating, offensive pigheadedness of the people in the kitchen, who had interpreted this to mean they could go ahead and cut up the fish into five.

"What the hell have they done!" Looking at the five slices of grilled fish (this was no longer sea bream, merely grilled fish) piled unimaginatively on the dish, I felt like crying. If they had at least served it raw as sashimi, I might have reconciled myself to it, I thought. Where were the head and the bones now? That big, splendid head—perhaps they had thrown it away! In this land of abundant fish, our hostelries no longer appreciate the finer points of seafood and do not have the least notion of how to prepare it.

"Don't get worked up. It's delicious," said the ever-affable N., calmly applying his chopsticks to the grilled fish.

"Really? Well then, why don't you eat the whole thing yourself? Go on, eat! I won't touch it. Are you fool enough to eat that stuff? It's all your fault! '*Remember! There's no need to divide it into three equal portions!*" It's because you had to explain everything in the contorted idiom of your Kanita town council budget meetings that that dimwit of a maid bungled it. It's your fault, and I won't forget it!"

N. chuckled.

"But don't you see the joke? When you tell them not to cut something into three pieces, they go and cut it into five. They're comedians, these people, real comedians. Well, cheers, cheers, cheers!"

I was forced to join him in this meaningless toast, and perhaps due to my resentment at the way they had treated my bream, I got frightfully drunk and became quite riotous, but I soon fell fast asleep, well before the others. Even now it exasperates me when I think of that sea bream. It was plain idiocy.

The next morning when we woke up it was still raining. We went downstairs, where the hotel staff told us that ferry services had been suspended that day too. We had no choice but to walk along the coast all the way to Tappi. We decided to leave as soon as the rain stopped and crawled back into bed, talking of this and that while waiting for the weather to clear up.

"Once upon a time there were two sisters," I began a fairy tale. These sisters had received an equal number of pine cones from their mother, and with these pine cones they had been told to cook rice and bean paste soup. The younger sister, who was niggardly and calculating, used the pine cones very frugally and put them into the oven one by one, but she couldn't even heat the soup, let alone cook the rice. The elder sister, a warm and generous girl, threw all her pine cones into the oven at once, without fussing. With the fire blazing she was able to cook the rice without trouble and have embers enough left to heat the soup.

"Do you know that story? It has a lesson for us; namely, let's have a drink! Didn't we put one container aside last night to take with us to Tappi? Let's finish that one. It won't do us any good to be stingy. This is no time to be fussy; let's polish it all off at once. Who can say that later there won't be any embers left? Maybe there won't be any need for them anyway. When we get to Tappi, we'll think of something. And if there's nothing to drink there, that doesn't matter, does it? It's not as if it would kill us to go to bed sober and meditate quietly on our past and our future."

"I see, I see!" N. jumped to his feet. "Let's do just like the elder sister. We'll polish it all off at once!"

We got out of bed and sat down around the sunken hearth, where we heated up the leftover *sake* in an iron kettle, and while we were waiting for the rain to stop we finished every last drop.

At about noon the rain stopped. We had a late breakfast and prepared to leave. It was chilly and overcast. In front of our inn we said goodbye to Mr. M., and then N. and I set off northward.

"Shall we go up and have a look?" N. had stopped at a stone arch in front of the Gikeiji temple.[8] The name of the donor of the arch, someone from Matsumae, was chiseled into one of its pillars.

We passed under the arch and climbed up the stone stairs. It was some way to the top. From the branches of the trees that lined the steps, drops of the morning's rain fell on our heads.

"Is this it?"

On the summit of the hill we found an ancient, weather-beaten temple with the bamboo-and-gentian crest of the Minamoto on its doors. For some reason I felt deeply disgusted and said again, "Is this it?"

"This is it," answered N. inanely.

> After his escape from Takadate, Minamoto no Yoshitsune had come this far and was about to cross to Ezo when he was delayed here for several days by unfavorable winds. Because of the urgency of the situation, he placed a statue

of Kannon that he was carrying with him on top of a rock in the sea and prayed for a fair wind. Instantly the wind changed direction, and he was able to cross to Matsumae without mishap. That statue is now in a temple here and is known as the Kannon to Which Yoshitsune Prayed for Wind.

This is the temple referred to in *Records of a Journey to the East*. We descended the stone steps in silence.

"Look, you see these little indentations on the steps? People say they're the footprints of Benkei, or of Yoshitsune's horses, or something," N. said, forcing a laugh. I wanted to believe the story, but I just could not.

When we passed back under the arch again, we saw a rock. Nankei says in his *Records*:

> There is, in addition, on the shore near Minmaya, a huge rock with three holes, one next to the other, like stables. Here Yoshitsune's horses were given shelter, and thus the place is known as Minmaya, Three-Horse Stable.

We deliberately passed by the enormous boulder as quickly as we could. There is something oddly embarrassing about finding that kind of legend in one's native land.

"My guess is that during the Kamakura period two young good-for-nothings drifted in from somewhere or other and tramped around conning the country girls. 'I must be frank with you and confess that I am Minamoto no Yoshitsune and that this bearded man here is Musashi-bō Benkei. We wish to be lodged for the night.' There are just too many legends about Yoshitsune in Tsugaru. For all I know, there were Yoshitsunes and Benkeis of that sort wandering around not just during the Kamakura period but in the Edo period too."

"Yes, but Benkei's job was a bit of a bore, wasn't it?" N.,

whose beard was much heavier than mine, appeared to be worried that he might be forced to play the part of Benkei. "Not much fun, carrying all that heavy armor around."

As we talked, we began to fantasize about how frightfully pleasant the vagrant life of those two young vagabonds must have been, and we became quite envious.

"There are a lot of pretty girls around here, don't you think?" I said quietly. In the villages we passed through, girls would dart out from behind the houses and disappear again immediately. Their white skin and neat clothes gave them an air of elegance and made it hard to believe that their hands and feet were worn with work.

"Huh? Oh, yes, now that you mention it. You're right." There are few men who get less worked up over women than N. He prefers a drink any time.

"If I were to introduce myself now as Yoshitsune, you don't think anyone would believe me, do you?" My imagination was running away with me.

When we began this silly conversation, we had been strolling along at an easy pace, but bit by bit we increased our tempo. It had almost become a contest to see who could walk faster and consequently we fell silent. The effect of the *sake* we had drunk in Minmaya had worn off. It was bitterly cold. We had no choice but to hurry along. We walked on briskly, with serious looks on our faces. The wind was gradually blowing stronger off the sea. Many times I thought my cap was going to be blown off my head, and each time I secured it by tugging at its peak, until finally I tore the rayon that connected peak to cap. At times big drops of rain fell. Dense black clouds hung low in the sky. The waves had swollen and spray stung our cheeks as we walked along the narrow road by the shore.

"Still, this road used to be much worse. You should have seen it six or seven years ago! In those days there were I don't know how many places where you had to wait for the waves to pull back and then rush across quickly. . . ."

"But even now it's no good at night, is it? No way of getting through."

"Right. At night it's not possible. Not even for Yoshitsune and Benkei."

Our faces took on a serious look as we discussed the road, and we started walking still faster.

"Aren't you getting tired?" said N., looking back over his shoulder. "Your legs are holding up better than I thought they would."

"I'm still young, you know."

After we had been walking for about two hours, the scenery around us began to look strangely desolate, and even, one might say, forbidding. It was no longer scenery. When you talk of scenery, you think of something that has been seen and described by many people over long periods of time. Human eyes have, as it were, softened it with their gaze, human hands have fed it and tamed it. Even the hundred-meter-high Kegon Falls has this vague smell of people about it, like a wild beast in a cage. In all the steep and rugged places that have ever been celebrated in paintings, songs, or poems, without a single exception, one can discover some human element, but this extreme northern coast of Honshu has steadfastly refused to transform itself into anything resembling scenery. It even spurns that speck of a human figure that can often be seen in landscape paintings. If one were to insist on sketching it in, one would have to use an old Ainu dressed in his white *attush*.[9] The canvas would simply refuse to accept a dandy in a purple jumper. This landscape does not lend itself to picture or song. There are just the rocks, and water.

I believe it's Goncharov who tells of an old sea dog of a captain crying out during a storm, "Hey! Come up on deck for a moment and look! How would you describe these waves? I'm certain you literary gentlemen have some splendid adjectives for them." And Goncharov looked at the waves, heaved a deep sigh, and spoke only one word: "Frightening."

Just as no adjective from prose or poetry springs to mind to describe ocean breakers or desert storms, so there is only one word that befits the rocks and sea along Honshu's most far-flung road, and that word is "frightening." From then on I averted my eyes and kept them trained on the ground at my feet.

We still had some thirty minutes walking left before we would reach Tappi when I let out a muted laugh.

"We shouldn't have finished up that *sake* after all! I can hardly imagine they'll have any at our lodgings in Tappi. And it's so damned cold," I added, grumbling in spite of myself.

"Yes, I was just thinking the same thing. If we continue a little while longer, we'll reach the house of an old acquaintance of mine, and if we're lucky, they might just have kept their *sake* rations. They don't drink in that family."

"Will you ask them, please?"

"Yes, we've just got to have some *sake*."

The acquaintance lived in the last hamlet before Tappi. N. took off his cap and went inside, and a few minutes later he came out again, trying his best to stifle his laughter.

"Fortune favors the wicked! They filled up a whole container. We have about a liter."

"See? There were still some embers left. Let's go."

Only a little further. Backs bent into the storm, we struggled on toward Tappi. I was just thinking how narrow the path had become when I suddenly found myself with my head stuck inside a chicken coop. For a moment I had no idea what had happened.

"Tappi," said N., his tone of voice different from before. "This?"

When I looked around more calmly, I saw that what I had imagined to be a chicken coop was really the hamlet of Tappi: tiny houses, huddled tightly together, supporting and protecting one another against the ferocious elements.

This is the end of Honshu. Beyond this hamlet there is no road. There is nothing but a drop to the sea. This is Honshu's blind alley. Mark my words, reader: if you walk north following the road, ever northward, northward, you cannot fail to reach the Sotogahama Road; it will grow narrower and narrower, but if you carry on northward, you will at last reach this strange, chicken-coop world, and there you will have come to the absolute end of your road.

"Everybody is amazed at first. The first time I came here I thought I had walked into someone's kitchen," said N.

However, the area is vital to our national defense, so I must be careful not to say anything else concerning this little village.

Turning up an alley, we arrived at our inn. An old woman appeared and showed us to our quarters. The rooms in this inn, too, were amazingly tidy, and the house itself was far from flimsy. The first thing we did was change into quilted dressing gowns and settle down on either side of the small sunken hearth. Ah, that felt a lot better!

"Oh, and do you have any *sake*?" inquired N. of the old woman in a relaxed tone that suggested he was a prudent and sensible person. The answer was unexpected.

"Yes, we do." She was an elegant old lady with a distinguished-looking oval face. She was perfectly composed as she answered us. N. forced a smile.

"No, I'm afraid I wasn't making myself clear. You see, we would like to drink quite a lot."

"Go ahead. There's as much as you like," she said smiling.

We looked at each other in surprise. Could it be that this old woman didn't know *sake* had become a precious commodity these days?

"We received our rations today, and since there are several places around here where the people don't drink, we collected it all together," she said, her hands making a gesture as if collecting, and then, spreading her arms wide as if to embrace a whole host of two-liter bottles: "A little while ago my husband came home carrying this much!"

"That should be plenty," I said, vastly relieved. "We'll warm them up in this kettle. Please bring us four or five flasks, would you? Or better still, make it six." I thought it best to order a lot before the old lady changed her mind. "You can bring the food later."

The old lady returned carrying a tray with the six flasks of *sake* we had asked for. Before we had finished the first two, the food appeared.

"Please help yourselves."

"Thank you."

The six flasks disappeared in no time.

"They're gone already!" I was dumbfounded. "That was ridiculously fast. Far too fast."

"Did we drink that much?" N., too, looked incredulous as he shook the empty flasks one by one. "Nothing. It's so damned cold we must have drunk them without being aware of it."

"All those flasks, they were all filled to overflowing. If we order six more after drinking these so fast, the old girl may think we're up to no good and put up her guard. She might say that we're frightening her and refuse to serve us any more—and we can't have that. We'd better heat up the *sake* we brought and drink that to make the interval seem longer, and then order another six flasks or so. Tonight, in this inn on the northern tip of Honshu, we'll drink the night away!" This strange stratagem proved to be our undoing.

We poured the *sake* from our container into the flasks and this time did our best to drink as slowly as we could. Before long, N. suddenly became quite drunk.

"This is terrible. I think I'm going to get drunk tonight."

It wasn't just a matter of him thinking he was going to get drunk, he looked horribly drunk already. "This is terrible. Tonight I'm going to get drunk. All right? Do you mind?"

"I don't care. I'm planning to get drunk myself. Let's just take it nice and easy."

"Suppose I sing a song? I don't think you've ever heard me sing. I hardly ever do. But tonight I want to sing a song. Hey, listen, mind if I sing?"

"Can't be helped. Let's hear it." And I braced myself.

" 'How many mountains and rivers . . .' " With eyes closed, N. softly sang Bokusui's traveling song. It wasn't as bad as I had expected. When I closed my eyes and listened, I felt quite touched.

"Well, was it that bad?"

"No, I actually felt moved."

"In that case, I'll sing another one."

This time it was awful. The visit to this inn at the northern tip of Honshu must have stirred N.'s spirit, for he raised a raucous bellow that was positively shocking.

" 'On the silver SHOOORe of an IIISlet in the EEEASTern SEEEA!' " he began a song by Takuboku, and his voice was so loud and wild that it completely drowned out the sound of the wind outside.

"Frightful!" I said.

"Frightful? Then I must see if I can't do any better."

After a deep breath, he erupted again. "On the islet of a shore in the eastern sea," he sang mistakenly, and then for some unknown reason suddenly came out with " 'Writing now my own account of past events,' " from the *Masukagami*. He groaned, he screamed, he howled; it really became rather disgusting. I was praying that the old lady downstairs might not hear it, but alas, the sliding doors opened, and there she was.

"Ah, I see you're singing! How about turning in by and by?" With these words she cleared away the trays and briskly spread out the bedding. She seemed genuinely shaken by N.'s magnificent roars. I had intended to do a lot more drinking, but the whole thing had become very stupid.

"Disgusting! Your singing was disgusting! You should've stopped after one or two. That performance was enough to frighten anyone." Grumbling and complaining, I resigned myself to the inevitable.

The next morning, still in bed, I heard the beautiful voice of a girl. The wind had died down, the morning sun shone into our room, and in the street in front of the house a young girl was singing a handball song. I raised my head and pricked up my ears.

> Sè sè sè.
> The eighty-eighth night
> And summer draws near.
> In mountains and meadows
> Wisteria waves ripple
> In the fresh green wind.
> Time for a game![10]

I had not expected to hear such a sweet song so beautifully enunciated here in the northern tip of Honshu, scorned as it still is as a land of barbarians by the people of central Japan. As Professor Satō wrote:

> Before one can discuss the Ōshū of today, one should recognize that it is imbued with the same pent-up energy that existed in Italy immediately before the Renaissance. Culture and industry have benefited from Emperor Meiji's interest in education, which rapidly made its influence felt even in Ōshū's remotest nooks and corners. The harsh nasal twang so characteristic of the speech of its people disappears as the standard language is promoted. The dwelling place of ignorant, barbarian tribes which once wallowed in the

mire of primitive conditions has received the bright light of education.''

I felt the dawning of a new day in the lilting voice of that girl, and I was moved beyond words.

1 (p. 64)   From *A Record of the Tenpō Famine* (*Tenpō kyōkō rokushō*). This passage, including the ellipsis, is quoted verbatim in Takeuchi Unpei's *History of Aomori Prefecture*, p. 277. The author of the note inserted in the text is uncertain.

2 (p. 65)   *Eighth Division.* This division was stationed in Hirosaki (see p. 18). During the war it fought in China, but was transferred to the Philippines just before the Battle of Leyte in December 1944.

3 (p. 70)   *Ezo.* Although not all Ezo were Ainu, Tachibana appears to assume they were. The names of the villages he cites are indeed of Ainu origin, as were the people of Utetsu, the home of the last Ainu of Honshu, who in 1756 were finally registered as Japanese.

4 (p. 74)   According to Mori's version of the legend, the children Anju and Zushiō leave their home in Iwaki province with their mother to search for their exiled father. At Naoe they fall into the hands of slave traders who part the children from their mother and sell them to Sanshō the Steward, a wealthy landowner in Tango. Sanshō makes the children work hard and ill-treats them in various ways. Finally Zushiō escapes, but Anju stays behind and drowns herself in a swamp. On Zushiō's arrival in Kyoto, his noble lineage is recognized and he secures a pardon for his father, only to find that he has died already. Zushiō is made governor of Tango and abolishes slavery there. At the end of the story he is reunited with his mother on the island of Sado.

5 (p. 75)   *Iwaki* and *Iwashiro* are written with different characters, but Iwaki (岩城) can easily be misread as Iwashiro. Mt. Iwaki in Tsugaru used to be written with the same characters as Iwaki Province, but has since normalized its spelling—insofar as such a phenomenon can be said to exist in Japanese orthography—from 岩城 to 岩木. Dazai is suggesting, in other words, that the legend originated in Iwashiro, became associated with Iwaki Province through a common spelling error, and thus found its way to Mt. Iwaki in Tsugaru.

6 (p. 81)   Because of the rhyme effect, sea bream (*tai*) is often served on congratulatory (*omedetai* or *arigatai*) occasions.

7 (p. 82)   Dazai's skepticism is warranted, for the historical forty-seven samurai all committed suicide in 1703. According to local tradition, they had taken the precaution to send a forty-eighth samurai to Kanita, to take over in case their original plot failed.

8 (p. 86)   *Gikeiji temple*. The characters *gi-kei* (義経) can also be read *yoshitsune*. Gikeiji is therefore the Yoshitsune Temple.

9 (p. 89)   *Attush*. The Ainu word for a coat of elm-bark fiber.

10 (p. 94)   Professor Sōma points out (pp. 219–20) that there is no such handball song, but that Dazai combined a tea-picking song with a counting song, presumably to create a contrast with N.'s raucous singing of the previous night.

The eighty-eighth night after the beginning of spring according to the lunar calendar was traditionally the day when the rice was sown. Nowadays it falls in early May (on May 2 in 1984).

IV

The Tsugaru Plain

Tsugaru. Traditional name for a region on the Japan Sea coast in the extreme northeast of the country. While on an expedition launched against the Ezo of Dewa during the reign of Empress Saimei [655–61], Abe no Hirafu, the governor of Koshi, progressed through Akita (then written with different characters) and Nushiro (the modern Noshiro) to Tsugaru, and finally to Hokkaido.

The name ''Tsugaru'' first occurs in a record stating that local chieftains had been put in charge of the Tsugaru region [655].

When Sakaibe no Muraji Iwashiki was sent on a mission to the Tang Court, he showed some Ezo tribesmen to the Chinese emperor [659]. In answer to the emperor's question concerning the various kinds of Ezo, Iki no Muraji Hakatoko, one of the officials in the ambassador's suite, explained that there were three tribes: those who lived nearest were called Nigi, or Soft, Ezo; then came the Ara, or Rough, Ezo; those who lived furthest away were called Tsugaru; and there was strong evidence to believe that there existed Ezo who belonged to still other tribes.

The Tsugaru Ezo are frequently mentioned in connection with the rebellion of the Ebisu of Dewa in 878. At that time the commander of the government troops was Fujiwara no Yasunori. In his campaign to suppress the rebellion he crossed from Tsugaru to Oshima where he subjected to Japanese rule several Ezo tribes who in the past had never acknowledged the authority of the central government. Oshima is now called Hokkaido.

It was not until Minamoto no Yoritomo had established control over the whole of the north of Honshu [1189] that Tsugaru was made a part of Mutsu Province.

Aomori Prefecture, History. Until the first years of the Meiji era [1868–1912], the area covered by this prefecture, together with the land now constituting the prefectures of Iwate, Miyagi, and Fukushima, formed one province, called Mutsu. Before Aomori was formally established as a prefecture, its territory had been divided into the feudal domains of Hirosaki, Kuroishi, Hachinohe, Shichinohe, and Tonami, but in the seventh month of 1871 these domains were dissolved and reorganized as prefectures. In the ninth month of the same year these prefectures were abolished and temporarily amalgamated into one new one, called Hirosaki Prefecture, which itself was dissolved and replaced by Aomori Prefecture two months later. All the above-mentioned domains fell under its jurisdiction, although later Ninohe County was appended to Iwate Prefecture. This is the situation as it exists today.

Tsugaru Family. Family descended from the Fujiwara. At the beginning of the twelfth century, Hideshige, an eighth-generation descendant of the military prefect Hidesato, ruled the Tsugaru region in Mutsu. Later he built a castle at the Tsugaru port of Jūsan and took Tsugaru as his family name. During the last decade of the fifteenth century, Masanobu, a son of Konoe Hisamichi, was adopted into the family, which rose to prominence under Masanobu's grand-

1. Tsushima Gen'emon, Dazai's father. "... if my father could have been spared a little longer, he might have been of much, much greater service to Tsugaru."

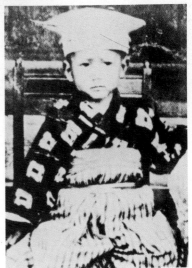

2. Dazai at age five. "You were a lot of trouble, but you were so sweet."

3. The Tsushima household at Yamagen, ca. 1925. Back row, right to left: Shūji, Eiji, Bunji, Reiji. Middle row, from right to left: Bunji's wife Rei, his sister Toshi with his daughter Yō, Tane, Ishi, Kie.

4. At Aomori Middle School. From left to right: Dazai, his brother Reiji, and Nakamura Teijirō (''N.'').

5. Farewell party for the graduating members of the Hirosaki Higher School Newspaper Club, ca. 1930. Front row, second from right: Dazai.

6. Dazai in a bar on the Ginza, autumn 1947.

7. Dazai at a railroad crossing near his house in Mitaka, shortly before his death in 1948.

8. Room in the Shayōkan. "In the best Japanese-style room in the house, the one with the gold leaf on the sliding doors, my brothers sat quietly drinking their *sake*—and then I burst in."

9. Garden of the Shayōkan, Dazai's old home. "In the afternoon I went out for a solitary walk and looked at the garden in the rain from under my umbrella."

10. Dream or reality? "So long as the trees near the pond bear a myriad flowers and its white-walled keep stands proud and silent, Hirosaki Castle will surely rank among the great castles of the world."

11. Train crossing the Tsutsumi River at Aomori. In the background, Mount Hakkōda.

12. Hirosaki Nebuta, 1906. "Young people, dressed up in all sorts of costumes, dance through the streets in a parade, pulling huge lanterns which are shaped like warriors, dragons, or tigers painted in brilliant colors, and mounted on wagons."

13. Fragment of a scroll in the Unshōji Temple, Kanagi. "Arsonists had baskets ablaze with red flames bound to their backs. . . ."

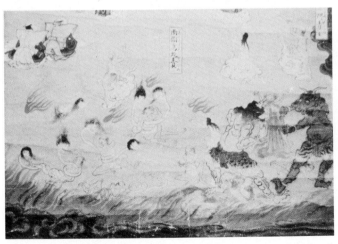

14. ". . . adulterers were crushed by two-headed, green snakes coiled around their bodies. . . ."

15. *Komohi* in Kizukuri. "If you think of the *komohi* of the north country as long passageways formed not by awnings but by permanent solid structures—the eaves of the houses extended a little forward—you will have a fairly accurate picture."

17. Athletic meet in Kodomari, with booths. "The men were drinking, the women and children were eating, and everyone was talking and laughing in the best of spirits."

16. Haikara-chō in Goshogawara, ca. 1925. "My aunt lives in Haikara-chō, the Smart Quarter."

18. Mount Iwaki as seen from Hirosaki Castle. "As I stood looking toward Mount Iwaki from a corner of the open space in front of the main keep, I suddenly noticed a dream town silently unfolding at my feet."

20. "... the drifts of snow would not melt and the farmers had to use sledges to carry the snow off their fields."

19. Aboard the Tsugaru Railroad, 1984.

21. The Japan Sea coast near Shariki. "We have an unobstructed view of Shichiri Nagahama, the Seven-League Strand. From Cape Gongen in the north to Cape Ōdose in the south there is nothing to interrupt the compass of our gaze."

22. Shimoyama Seiji ("Mr. S."), at home in Kanagi. "Mr. S. was getting merrier and merrier."

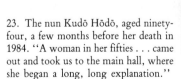

23. The nun Kudō Hōdō, aged ninety-four, a few months before her death in 1984. "A woman in her fifties . . . came out and took us to the main hall, where she began a long, long explanation."

24. Take in old age. "Perhaps I am biased, but it seems to me that Take is a cut above the other *aba* of this village."

25. Nakamura Teijirō, Koshino Take, and Nakabata Keikichi at the unveiling of the Dazai Memorial in Ashino Park, Kanagi, in 1965. The inscription is a translation of one of Dazai's favorite lines: "J'ai l'extase et j'ai la terreur d'être choisi," (Verlaine, "Sagesse").

son Tamenobu. Tamenobu's descendants established separate branches, one ruling the former domain of Hirosaki, and the other, the former Kuroishi domain.

Tsugaru Tamenobu. Sixteenth-century warlord. His father was Ōura Jinzaburō Morinobu, and his mother, the daughter of Takeda Shigenobu, Lord of Horikoshi Castle. He was born in the first month of 1550 and received the childhood name Ōgi. In the third month of 1567, when he was eighteen years old, he was adopted by his uncle, Tsugaru Tamenori, and became the protégé of Konoe Sakihisa. His wife was Tamenori's daughter. In the fifth month of 1571 he met Nanbu Takanobu in battle and killed him. On the twenty-seventh of the seventh month of 1578 he attacked Kitabatake Akimura, Lord of Namioka Castle, and annexed his territory. He proceeded to seize many of the villages in that area, and by 1585 had unified all of Tsugaru. In 1587 he set out to join forces with Toyotomi Hideyoshi, but Abe Sanesue, Lord of Akita, barred his passage south and forced him to return. In 1589 he sent hawks and horses to Hideyoshi as a token of friendship, and he was quick to join Hideyoshi at the Siege of Odawara in 1590. Consequently, he was confirmed as "Lord of all Tsugaru and Sotogahama." In 1591 he also sent soldiers to help suppress the Kunohe rebellion. In the fourth month of 1593 he went to Kyoto and was granted an audience with Hideyoshi. He also visited the Konoe family and obtained permission to use its peony family emblem. He then sent soldiers to join Hideyoshi's army at Nagoya in Hizen. In the first month of 1594 he was promoted to the Junior Fourth Rank, Lower Grade, and given the post of Steward of Eastern Kyoto. At the Battle of Sekigahara in 1600, he sent soldiers to support the cause of Tokugawa Ieyasu. He fought at Ōgaki and had his revenue increased by two thousand *koku* when he was granted the fief of Ōdate in Kō-zuke. On the fifth day of the twelfth month of 1607 he died in Kyoto, at the age of fifty-eight.

Tsugaru Plain. Plain in Mutsu Province, covering the counties of South, Central, and North Tsugaru. It is the basin of the Iwaki River. Its eastern border is formed by the mountain ridge that runs from the west of Lake Towada northward up the Tsugaru Peninsula. To the south it extends as far as the watershed that forms the border with Ugo and is marked by the stone at Yatate Pass. On the west side it is protected by the mass of Mt. Iwaki and the dunes along the coast (popularly called the Screen Hills). The Iwaki River itself flows from the west and is joined north of Hirosaki by the Hira River, which flows from the south, and the Ase'ishi River, which flows from the east. Together the waters of these rivers flow due north and empty into the Jūsan Lagoon, and so into the sea. From north to south the extent of the plain is approximately sixty kilometers; its width from east to west is approximately twenty kilometers. The plain grows narrower to the north: at its widest point it measures about twelve kilometers, but at the coast of the Jūsan Lagoon it is a mere four kilometers in width. The area between these points is a low-lying plain crisscrossed by a maze of tributary waterways. Most of the rice in Aomori Prefecture is grown in this plain.

(From the *Great Japanese Encyclopedia*)

Most people know little about the history of Tsugaru. It seems some even think Tsugaru is the same thing as Mutsu Province or Aomori Prefecture. This is hardly surprising. In the textbooks on Japanese history that we used at school, Tsugaru was mentioned only once, and that was in passing, in connection with

Abe no Hirafu's subjugation of the Ezo: "After Emperor Kōtoku died, Empress Saimei ascended the throne; Prince Naka no Ōe, now Crown Prince, assisted her in the government of the Realm; he sent Abe no Hirafu to pacify the regions that are now known as Akita and Tsugaru [658]." This passage mentions Tsugaru, but there is no reference to Tsugaru anywhere else, either in our elementary school textbooks, or in middle school textbooks, or even in lectures at higher schools.

The legendary expedition of the four generals of 88 B.C. is said to have penetrated as far north as present-day Fukushima Prefecture, and about two hundred years later Prince Yamato Takeru's campaign against the Ezo apparently took.him even further north, to Hidakami, which was probably the northern part of Miyagi Prefecture. About 510 years pass before we arrive at the Taika Reform [645], after which the name of Tsugaru is first mentioned in connection with Abe no Hirafu's subjection of the Ezo and then disappears again. It is said that Taga Castle (near modern Sendai) and Akita Castle were built, in 724 and 733 respectively, to control the Ezo, but no mention is made of Tsugaru. In 794, and again in 801, Sakanoue no Tamuramaro advanced far to the north, destroyed the strongholds of the Ezo, and built Izawa Castle (near modern Mizusawa in Iwate Prefecture) to keep the region under control, but he does not seem to have penetrated as far as Tsugaru. Later there was the campaign by Fumiya no Watamaro [812], and the year 878 saw the rebellion of the Dewa Ezo against which Fujiwara no Yasunori mounted his campaign. It is said that the Tsugaru Ezo may have supported this rebellion. But the only name which we nonexperts in history associate with Ezo campaigns is that of Sakanoue no Tamuramaro. After that, we skip 250 years to the beginning of the period dominated by the Minamoto and Taira families, to learn about the Earlier Nine Years' War and the Later Three Years' War. Our textbooks state only that these wars were fought in modern Iwate and Akita prefectures, and that the so-called Nigi, or Soft, Ezo of the Abe and Kiyohara families played an active part in them, but about the movements of the pure Ezo of the hinterland, the Tsugaru, they say nothing at all. Then came the one hundred years and more of splendor under the three generations of the Fujiwara at Hiraizumi, and the subjugation of the whole of the northeast by Minamoto no Yoritomo in 1189, but our textbooks steadily ignore the north of the country. The Satsuma, Chōshū, and Tosa domains were actively involved in the Meiji Restoration, but to the various domains of Ōshū the event meant no more, it would seem, than a momentary getting up to rearrange their kimonos and then sitting down again. For this backward yet opportunistic behavior they are often taken to task. But what else, we must ask, could they have done? In the last analysis—nothing at all.

It fills me with sadness to think that our textbooks treat the Age of the Gods with great awe, but only mention the name of Tsugaru once in all those years between the Emperor Jinmu and the present, and then only in connection with Abe no Hirafu. What on earth were they doing in Tsugaru all those years? Just getting up to rearrange their kimonos and then sitting down again, all the time, for twenty-six hundred years, without taking one step outside their own borders, just blinking their eyes? No, no— that can't have been the case at all. If you asked the people themselves, they would answer: "That's how it might seem, but we were pretty busy, you know."

The name Ōu is a combination of Ōshū and Dewa, and Ōshū is a shortened form for the name Mutsushū. Mutsu was the general name for the country north of the barriers of Shirakawa and Nakoso. Its real name was Michi-no-Oku, the End of the Road, but this was abbreviated to Michinoku, and, with the word *michi*, road, being pronounced *mutsu* in the old regional dialect, it became Mutsu Province. This is where the Eastern Sea Road and the Eastern Mountain Road ended and where the remotest foreign tribes lived, so it quite naturally came to be called the End of the Road. The character used to write *mutsu* here, is usually pronounced *riku*, land.[1]

The name Dewa comes from *ideha* and can be taken to mean *idehashi*, frontier. In olden days people referred to the region along the Japan Sea coast northeast of the mountains of central Honshu as Koshi, the Other Side. The country beyond Koshi was, like Michinoku, long inhabited by uncivilized foreign tribes, and that is probably why it was called the Frontier, to indicate that together with Michinoku on the Pacific side it was a remote land that had long remained independent of imperial rule.

This is what Professor Kida has to say, and he is brevity itself. Explanations should be nothing if not clear and to the point. Dewa and Ōshū were regarded as remote and uncivilized lands, and as for the Tsugaru Peninsula beyond them in the extreme north, perhaps it was thought of as a region inhabited by bears and monkeys. About the history of Ōu, Professor Kida adds the following:

Although Yoritomo had subjugated Ōu, he was of course unable to govern it in the same way he did his other territories. Instead, he asserted that "Dewa and Mutsu are Ebisu country," and used that as an excuse for not fully implementing his land reform policy and for ordering that all the old laws of Hidehira and Yasuhira be observed. He had virtually no other option. Consequently, seeing that regions like Tsugaru in the extreme north, where many of the people still followed their old Ezo ways, were difficult even for Kamakura warriors to bring under control, he appointed the powerful local Andō family as governors and supervisors of the Ezo, and thus pacified the region.

From about the time of the Andō we begin to learn a little about Tsugaru. Before that, for all we know, only the Ainu wandered aimlessly. But these Ainu are not to be looked down on. They form one of the so-called ancestral races of the Japanese people and seem to have been of a quite different disposition than the dispirited remnants of the Ainu in Hokkaido today. What we know of their pottery suggests that it was superior to that of Stone Age people in other parts of the world.

The ancestors of the modern Hokkaido Ainu have lived on the island since earliest times. They had little contact with the culture of Honshu. Their land was isolated, it had few of the blessings of nature. Not even in the Stone Age therefore did they achieve the degree of development we see in their Ōu cousins. Especially in more recent times, after the establishment of the Matsumae domain [1601], they were often subjected to oppression by the Japanese. This weakened them severely and reduced them to an extreme degree of degradation. The Ainu of Ōu, on the other hand, while taking a vigorous pride in their independent culture, either emigrated to the provinces of Japan proper or intermarried with the many Japanese settlers who came to Ōu, until at last the two peoples were indistinguishable. The geography professor Ogawa Takuji comes to the following conclusion:

The *Shoku-Nihongi* records how in the early and late Nara periods the Shukushin and people from Parhae crossed the Japan Sea to Japan. The most remarkable years were 746 under Emperor Shōmu and 771 under Emperor Kōnin, when large groups of people from Parhae, the first group numbering more than one thousand and the second over three hundred, arrived in what is now the Akita region; from this it can be inferred that traffic to and from Manchuria moved with great freedom. There have been archeological finds of Chinese copper coins of the early Han dynasty near Akita, and it seems that somewhere in the northeast there was a shrine dedicated to the Han Emperors Wen-ti and Wu-ti. Each of these facts lends great credibility to the conjecture that there existed direct contact between the continent and that region. In the *Konjaku Monogatari* there is an account of how Abe no Yoritoki crossed to Manchuria, and if one considers all the information provided by archeology and folklore, this should not be dismissed as just a story.[2] We can go one step further and feel confident that the level of civilization attained by the savage northeastern tribes as a result of direct contact with the continent before the eastward expansion of imperial rule was not as low as we are led to believe from the insufficient historical data that have survived in Central Japan. It is difficult to understand why it cost generals like Tamuramaro, Yoriyoshi, and Yoshi'ie such mighty efforts to subdue these tribes if one fails to realize that their bravery was not the result of mere ignorance, as is the case with the Taiwanese aborigines.[3]

Professor Ogawa adds that it is interesting to speculate whether the governors appointed by the imperial court who adopted names for themselves such as Ezo, Easterner, or Hairy One, did so because they wished to be as valorous as the people of Ōu, or because they wanted to enjoy the luxury of a chic, exotic name. Bearing all this in mind, it would seem that the ancestors of the Tsugaru people were certainly not just wandering aimlessly here at Honshu's northern tip, even though mainstream history never explains satisfactorily exactly who they were or what they did.

From the time of the aforementioned Andō family, our picture of Tsugaru becomes a little less murky. Professor Kida writes:

> The Andō referred to themselves as descendants of Abe no Sadatō's son Takaboshi and claimed Nagasune-hiko's elder brother Abi as their distant ancestor. When Nagasune-hiko

was killed fighting Emperor Jinmu, his brother Abi was exiled to Sotogahama in Ōshū, and the Abe were said to have been his descendants. However that may be, the Andō were undoubtedly a very powerful family in northern Ōu, even before the Kamakura period.

The three inner districts of Tsugaru were Kamakura fiefs, and the three outer districts crown domains. That this region was nevertheless not listed in the Register of Revenues and was thus exempted from tax levies is said to prove that the influence of the Kamakura shogunate did not extend to this remote part of the country, and that it was left to the Andō to do with as they pleased, a so-called immune estate.

Toward the end of the Kamakura period there was discord within the Andō family, which finally resulted in an uprising of the Ezo. The Hōjō Regent Takatoki sent a general to put it down, but he was unsuccessful, even with all the might of the Kamakura samurai on his side, and finally he negotiated a peace and withdrew.

When discussing the history of Tsugaru, even an expert like Professor Kida shows at times that he is not completely sure of himself. So it seems that in the history of Tsugaru there is still much that remains unclear. There is only one thing that does appear to be certain, and that is that this northernmost province never lost in its fights with other provinces. The idea of submission to outsiders seems to have been absolutely lacking. Warlords in other parts of the country had apparently given it up as hopeless and turned a blind eye, leaving Tsugaru to shift for itself—not unlike a certain contemporary writer. Be that as it may, because other provinces refused to oblige them, the people of Tsugaru began to malign one another and to fight among themselves. The agitation among the Tsugaru Ezo that originated in the Andō family feud is an example. According to Takeuchi Unpei's *History of Aomori Prefecture*:

> The discord among the Andō caused disturbances in the Kantō region and ultimately, in the words of the *Chronicle of the Nine Generations of Hōjō Regents*, "the beginning of the crisis that was to topple the government of the realm." Before long it led to the Genkō uprising and the restoration of Emperor Go-Daigo [1333].

Maybe, then, the Andō feud deserves mention as one of the causes of Emperor Go-Daigo's noble undertaking. If this is really the case, it is the only time that Tsugaru ever influenced, however remotely, the political situation in Central Japan, and the Andō family feud will have to be written with capital letters as one of the most glorious events in the annals of Tsugaru history.

The region on the Pacific side of modern Aomori Prefecture used to be inhabited by Ezo and had always been called Nuka-no-Bu, the Rice-Bran Region. At the beginning of the Kamakura period, the Nanbu family, a cadet branch of the Takeda clan of Kōshū, moved to Nuka-no-Bu, where their power grew and grew until it reached enormous proportions. The Yoshino and Muromachi periods passed, and until Hideyoshi brought the whole country under one rule, Tsugaru pitted itself against Nanbu. In Tsugaru, the Andō gave way to the Tsugaru family, who somehow managed to get themselves enfeoffed with the whole region and ruled over it for twelve successive generations until Lord Tsuguakira returned his fief to the emperor at the time of the Meiji Restoration. This, in a nutshell, is the history of Tsugaru.

There are several theories concerning the earliest forebears of the Tsugaru family. Professor Kida touches on this too:

> In Tsugaru, the Andō collapsed, the Tsugaru family ruled

alone, and there was a long period of hostility between them and the Nanbu along their joint border. It is said the Tsugaru are descended from the chancellor Konoe Hisamichi, but it is also said that they are descendants of Fujiwara no Motohira's second son Hideshige, and that they may be a branch of the Andō. Opinion is so divided that it is hard to know what to believe.

And Takeuchi Unpei has this to say:

All through the Edo period, relations between the Tsugaru and Nanbu families were remarkably hostile. One reason for this was that the Nanbu regarded the Tsugaru as ancestral enemies who had forcibly deprived them of their old territories; they maintained that the Tsugaru were originally a branch of the Nanbu who had turned on their lord in spite of their status as vassals. On the other hand, the Tsugaru claimed that their distant ancestors were Fujiwara, and that to this pedigree in the fifteenth century the blood of the Konoe had been added. It all.seems to stem from these claims. Of course, it is a fact that Nanbu Takanobu was killed by Tsugaru Tamenobu and a number of castles in the Tsugaru region that sided with the Nanbu were seized. In addition, the mother of Tamenobu's ancestor Ōura Mitsunobu was the daughter of the titular governor of Bizen, a Nanbu from Kuji, whose descendants several generations later held the courtesy title of governor of Shinano. Thus, I think it hardly surprising that the Nanbu considered the Tsugaru a race of traitors and harbored a deep resentment against them.

Now, as for the Tsugaru, they claim descent from the Fujiwara and Konoe families, but from a modern point of view they do not come armed with convincing evidence. The *Kasoku Chronicle* contends that they were not descended from the Nanbu, but its line of argument is extremely weak. According to the *Takaya Family Chronicle*, an old Tsugaru document, the Ōura family was a branch of the Nanbu, and the *Kidate Diary* says that "the houses of the Lords of Nanbu and of Tsugaru were one." Further, in the recently published *Companion to History* it is suggested that Tamenobu belonged to the Kuji branch of the Nanbu family; there is at present no definitive material to contradict this view. But even if the Tsugaru were of the same lineage as the Nanbu and used to be their vassals, it cannot be stated that their blood was not mixed with that of other noble families.

Like Professor Kida, Mr. Takeuchi refuses to commit himself. The only authority that provided an unambiguous explanation in plain and simple language was the *Great Japanese Encyclopedia*, which is why I opened this chapter with some excerpts from it.

All this has become quite tedious, and the whys and wherefores of Tsugaru pale into insignificance when considered from a national perspective. In his *Narrow Road to a Far Land* Bashō writes about his departure: "My heart grew heavy at the thought of the thousands of miles that lay ahead." But even so this led him no further north than Hiraizumi, on the southern border of what is now Iwate Prefecture. To reach Aomori Prefecture you must walk twice that distance, and then you must continue until you reach the solitary peninsula on the Japan Sea side of the prefecture: that is Tsugaru.

The spacious Tsugaru Plain, through which the Iwaki River runs most of its eighty-seven-kilometer course, was at the center of the Tsugaru domain. Its eastern boundary was the Aomori-Asamushi region; its western boundary, the Japan Sea coast from Cape Tappi in the north as far south as Fukaura; and I suppose you could say its southern boundary was Hirosaki. The cadet branch of Kuroishi had its territory between Hirosaki and the border with Akita, but that area has traditions peculiar to the

Kuroishi domain. A "cultural character" different from that of Tsugaru seems to have developed there, so we will pass it by. Tsugaru's northernmost point is Tappi. From top to bottom and side to side it doesn't amount to much—the whole is depressingly small. It is hardly surprising that it remained outside the mainstream of Japanese history.

At the absolute end of the End of the Road I spent one night, and because the next day there still was no sign that the boats would sail, we walked back the way we had come the day before, until we reached Minmaya. There we ate lunch and then got on a bus that took us straight back to N.'s home in Kanita. If you are on foot, Tsugaru is a lot larger than you think.

About noon two days later I left Kanita on board a ferry and arrived in Aomori harbor at about three o'clock in the afternoon. I took the Ōu trunk line to Kawabe, changed there for the Goshogawara-Noshiro line, and arrived in Goshogawara around five o'clock. I changed trains again straightaway and traveled north through the Tsugaru Plain on the Tsugaru Railroad. By the time I arrived in my native town of Kanagi it was already getting dark. As the crow flies, Kanita and Kanagi are not far apart, but they are separated by the Bonju Mountains, and since there is apparently no road across them worthy of the name, one has no choice but to make a huge detour and travel three sides of a square.

When I arrived at the house where I was born, I went first to the room with the family altar. My sister-in-law came with me and opened up the room. For a while I gazed at the photographs of my father and mother, and then bowed deeply. After that I went to the family living room and greeted my sister-in-law once again.

"When did you leave Tokyo?" she asked.

A few days before my departure I had sent her a postcard: I was leaving for a tour of Tsugaru and would stop by in Kanagi on the way to pay my respects at my parents' grave; would they mind putting me up for a few days?

"About a week ago. I was held up on the east coast. N. in Kanita was really good to me." I assumed someone had told her about N.

"Really? We got your postcard, but when you didn't show up we began to get worried that something might have happened to you. Yōko and Mitsuyo were waiting and waiting and took turns going to the station every day to see whether you had arrived. Finally they got upset and said they didn't want to see you if you did come."

Yōko is my eldest brother's eldest daughter. About six months earlier she had married a landowner from near Hirosaki. Apparently she often visits Kanagi with her husband, and on this occasion they were both there. Mitsuyo is our eldest sister's youngest daughter, a sweet-tempered girl who is still single and always comes to the Kanagi house to help. The two of them now appeared, arm in arm and giggling comically, to pay their respects to their shiftless sot of an uncle. Yōko seemed much more like a schoolgirl than a married woman.

"How funny you look!" They burst into laughter as soon as they saw my outfit.

"Don't laugh! This is all the rage in Tokyo."

Helped along by my sister-in-law, my grandmother appeared. She was then eighty-eight.

"I'm glad you came, oh, I'm so glad you came!" she said in a firm voice. She used to be full of vigor, but the years were beginning to tell.

"What will you do?" my sister-in-law asked me. "Will you eat here? Everyone else is upstairs."

My two brothers had already begun drinking upstairs with Yōko's husband, the guest of honor.

I was not quite certain yet what degree of decorum should be preserved between older and younger brothers, or to what extent I could forget formalities and be myself.

"If they have no objections, I guess I'll go upstairs." I hated the thought of sitting here drinking beer all by my wretched self.

"Whatever you like. I'm sure they won't mind," my sister-in-law said with a smile, and then, to Mitsuyo and Yōko, "Why don't you take a tray upstairs?"

Still dressed in my jumper, I went upstairs. In the best Japanese-style room in the house, the one with the gold leaf on the sliding doors, my brothers sat quietly drinking their *sake*—and then I burst in:

"I'm Shūji. Nice to meet you." First I greeted Yōko's husband, and then I apologized to my brothers for not having kept in touch. They grunted and gave the slightest of nods. That is our family style, or rather, perhaps I should say, that is our Tsugaru style. I'm used to it, so I calmly knelt down behind my tray and, served by Mitsuyo and my sister-in-law, drank my *sake* and kept quiet. Yōko's husband sat leaning against the alcove pillar, already pretty red in the face. My brothers used to be quite strong drinkers, but recently they seem to hold their liquor rather less well. They were "after you-ing" each other with impeccable politeness: "Come now, please, one more cup!" "No, really, I couldn't! But how about you? Please." My drinking in Sotogahama had been much more rough-mannered, and I was so startled at the difference between my brothers' way of life and my own that I felt as if I were in the palace of the Fairy Queen or on some other planet. I began to feel nervous.

"How about the crab? Later?" my sister-in-law whispered to me. I had brought some crab from Kanita as a present.

"Hmm." There is something a bit too rustic about crab that would tend to degrade such elegant trays, so I hesitated for a moment. Perhaps my sister-in-law felt the same way.

"Crab?" My eldest brother had overheard what we were talking about. "Don't worry. Just bring it up. And don't forget the napkins."

He appeared to be in a good mood, perhaps because his son-in-law was there.

The crab was served.

"Do start, help yourself," my brother urged his son-in-law, and was himself the very first to get down to work on the shells.

I felt much better.

"I'm sorry, but we haven't been properly introduced," Yōko's husband said to me with an unaffected smile on his face. I was momentarily taken aback, but then realized he was quite right.

"Well, you see, I'm Eiji's younger brother," I answered with a smile (Eiji is my second eldest brother), but then I had a disturbing thought: had it been all right to mention Eiji by name? I checked his face, but he looked completely blank, which left me with nothing to go by. Oh well, must be O.K., I thought, and shifted from my knees to a more comfortable cross-legged position. I had Mitsuyo pour me a beer for a change.

The very thought of my Kanagi home makes me feel tired. True, but do I really have to put that down in writing? The gods spare no love for a man who goes burdened under the bad karma of having to sell manuscripts filled with details of his family in order to earn a living; they banish him from his birthplace. I'm afraid I am doomed to move from one drab Tokyo dwelling to another, wandering around aimlessly, longing for my native home in my dreams, until at last I die.

The next day it was raining. I got up and went to my eldest brother's living room upstairs, where he was showing some paintings to his son-in-law, Yōko's husband. There were two gold-coated folding screens depicting quietly refined landscapes, one with wild cherries, the other a pastoral mountain scene with a river.

I looked at the painter's signature, but could not read it.

"Who painted this?" I asked, blushing nervously.

"Suian," my brother answered.

"Suian," I intoned, still in the dark.

"Don't you know him?" my brother inquired gently—it was not a reprimand. "He's the father of Hyakusui."

"Really?" I had heard that Hyakusui's father had also been a painter. That much I knew, but I knew neither that his name was Suian, nor that he had painted so well. I don't dislike paintings; on the contrary, I regard myself as something of a connoisseur, and that I knew nothing of Suian was a major lapse. Had I but cast a glance at the screen and said casually: "Isn't that a Suian?" my brother might perhaps have revised his opinion of me a little. But instead I go and blurt out: "Who painted this?" I squirmed at the thought that the damage was now irreparable, but my brother wasn't bothered.

"They have great artists in Akita," he said softly to his son-in-law.

"What do you think of our own Ayatari?" I put in timidly in an attempt to restore my reputation and to pander to my brother. So far as Tsugaru painters are concerned, it seems more or less to boil down to Ayatari. But I must admit I had not really known we possessed such a great painter in Tsugaru until my previous visit to Kanagi, when my brother showed me an Ayatari he owned.

"That's another story," my brother muttered in a tone that suggested he was not at all interested, and sat down in a chair. We had all been standing while we admired the screen painting, but when my brother sat down, his son-in-law took the chair facing his, while I sat down a little farther away, on the sofa near the door.

"This Suian now, I'd say he's more of an orthodox artist," he said, looking toward his son-in-law. For some reason it has never been his habit to address me directly.

114

It is true that Ayatari's brushwork is so thick and heavy that one senses his work would have sunk to the level of folk craft if he had carried it any further.

"Cultural traditions . . ." My brother hunched his back and looked his son-in-law straight in the face. ". . . I think you'll find they're more deeply rooted in Akita."

"Tsugaru's no good?" No matter what I said, the result would be gauche, so I had stopped caring and, with a smile, expressed my thoughts out loud.

"Didn't you say you were writing something about Tsugaru this time?" Suddenly my brother was talking directly to me.

"Yes, well, that's to say, I don't really know very much about Tsugaru." I became hopelessly flustered. "You don't happen to have any good reference books, do you?"

"Well," my brother laughed, "I'm not very interested in local history."

"Not even one of those really elementary books, *A Guide to Famous Places in Tsugaru*, or something like that? I'm really quite ignorant. . . ."

"I have nothing, nothing." My brother shook his head, smiling wryly as if appalled at my sloppy preparation. He got up and turned to his son-in-law.

"Well, I'm off to the Farmers' Association. Why not take a look through those books over there? Bad weather today anyway." And he left.

"I suppose they're pretty busy at the Farmers' Association these days," I said to Yōko's husband.

"Yes, just now they're deciding the rice delivery quota, so they've got their hands full." Despite his youth, he is a landowner and knows what he's talking about. He gave me an explanation with all sorts of detailed figures half of which I didn't understand.

"Until now I'd never really thought seriously about the importance of rice, and yet, in troubled times like these, when I look at the rice fields from the train window, I feel quite moved, as if they belonged to me personally. Won't the planting have to be delayed this year, now that it looks as if the weather's going to stay this cold?" As usual I had to show off my two cents' worth of knowledge in front of an expert.

"I expect it'll be all right. It really is pretty cold these days, but we'll think of something. The seedlings appear to be growing, oh, normally, I'd say."

"Is that so? . . . ." I nodded knowingly. "I noticed something from my train window yesterday that was a bit odd. I believe they call it horse-drawn plowing, when a horse is harnessed to the plow, but it seems most people now are using oxen for the job. When we were kids, we used horses not only for plowing, but also to draw carts and anything you could think of—horses for everything, and hardly ever oxen. The first time I ever saw an ox-drawn cart was when I went to Tokyo, and it struck me as positively weird."

"I can imagine. But horses have become very rare. Most of them have been sent to the front. And I suppose it also has something to do with the fact that oxen are easier to keep. Still, oxen are only half as efficient as horses, no, perhaps much worse than that."

"Speaking of being sent to the front . . ."

"You mean me? I've been called up twice, but both times, I'm ashamed to say, I was packed off back home." It was a pleasure to observe this healthy lad with his carefree, smiling face. "Next time I don't want to be sent back. . . ." He had a simple, natural way of speaking, and I enjoyed asking him questions.

"Aren't there any really good men hidden away in this part of the country, men you could call great and respect with all your heart?"

"Well, I wouldn't know about that, but perhaps, if you were lucky, you might just find one among the exemplary farmers."

"Perhaps you're right." I knew exactly what he meant. "I can't explain it very well, but I have this obsession about going through life as a—well—exemplary author, you might say. But my stupid vanity has turned me into a common snob, so I'll never make it. And as for these exemplary farmers, if you keep on telling them how exemplary they are, won't it spoil them?"

"It will. Yes, it will. Take the newspapers. They don't give a thought to the consequences when they make all this fuss about them, drag them away from their farms, make them give lectures, and so on, but it'll turn the head of even the best of them. When a person becomes famous, it spoils him."

"Absolutely!" Here again, I shared his feelings. "Men are sorry creatures who give in easily to glory. This journalism business started as an invention of American capitalists; that's why it takes nothing very seriously. It's poison: no sooner are you famous than you turn into a fool." It was a strange occasion to vent my indignation at my own fate. But let the reader beware. Deep in their hearts grumblers like me really want to be famous, no matter what they say.

In the afternoon I went out for a solitary walk and looked at the garden in the rain from under my umbrella. It was as if not a single tree or plant had changed, and I sensed that my brother must have made more than ordinary efforts to preserve the old house in its original state.

As I was standing near the pond, I heard a little "splish." I looked up: it was a frog jumping into the water, a trivial, slight sound. Suddenly I understood Bashō's haiku about the old pond. I had never been able to appreciate that poem. I had never been able to see what was so good about it. There's never anything special about famous things, I had concluded, but that was because my education had been at fault. What kind of explanation had they given us at school about the haiku of the old pond? In a shady corner lies a venerable old pond, they had told us. On a

117

still afternoon, SPLASH! (it sounds more like someone throwing himself into a river) a frog dives into the water. Aaah, the lingering echo! This is what another poet must have meant when he wrote, "When a lone bird breaks into song, the hills sound even stiller."[4]

That was what we were taught. What a pretentious, trite piece of doggerel! I thought it was so revolting that for a long time I wanted to have nothing to do with it, but now I had to admit I was wrong. If you begin your explication with a loud splash, you miss the point. And there is no echo, nor anything else. Instead it's best to start from that light "splish," the slenderest of sounds, so to speak, in some tucked-away corner of the world. A feeble sound. When Bashō heard it, he was touched.

Furu'ike ya	An old pond
Kawazu tobikomu	A frog jumps in
Mizu no oto	Sound of water

Read the poem again with this in mind and it's far from bad. In fact it's admirable! It succeeds in tossing overboard all the pretentious mannerisms of the Danrin school. The idea itself is unconventional: there is no moon, no snow, no flowers; there is no artistic elegance either, just the poor life of a poor creature. I can well understand why this haiku appalled the arbiters of taste: it signified the collapse of the traditional concept of elegance. It was revolutionary.

That night, all excited by the realization that it is a lie to say that a good artist must follow the beaten track, I wrote in my travel diary: "*Yamabuki ya / Kawazu tobikomu / Mizu no oto* [Yellow roses / A frog jumps in / Sound of water]. Who cares a rap about Kikaku? He's got no idea what it's all about.[5] *Ware to kite / Asobe ya oya no / Nai suzume* [Come with me / And play / Little sparrow orphan].[6] That's more like it, but it's too direct, really. 'An old pond' is peerless."

The next day the weather was beautiful. Four of us—my niece Yōko, her husband, myself, and Aya, who carried our lunch—went for a picnic on Takanagare, a gently sloping hill not quite two hundred meters high, some four kilometers east of Kanagi. "Aya" is not a girl's name, though it sounds like one; it means something like "grandpa," but it is also used to mean "father." The feminine form of *aya* is *apa*, sometimes pronounced *aba*. I, for one, have no idea where these words come from. One guess is that they are dialect forms of *oya*, parent, and *oba*, aunt, but that doesn't really get us much further. Indeed, there seem to be as many explanations proposed as there are proponents. According to my niece, the name of the hill, Takanagare, High Stream, should by rights be Takanagane, Long High Root, for it slopes down gently over its whole length, exactly like a long root; but I suppose in this case, too, the explanation changes with the explainer. The peculiar charm of the study of local lore seems to lie in the very fact that everyone has a different version and you never know which one is right.

As Yōko and Aya were still busy preparing our lunch, I left the house ahead of them with Yōko's husband. The weather was fine. May and June are the best months to travel in Tsugaru. *Records of a Journey to the East* concurs:

> People have always traveled to the northern districts in summer only, when plants and trees wear a fresh green garb, breezes blow from the south, the sea presents a tranquil mien, and the region belies its fearful reputation, but my journey to the north occupied the time between the ninth and third months, and I did not meet a single traveler on my way. Since I was journeying in the pursuit of medical knowledge, my case was different, but I strongly advise those who travel merely out of a desire to see famous places to visit this province after the fourth month.

These are the words of an experienced traveler, and my readers had better take them to heart. In Tsugaru the apricot, peach, cherry, apple, pear, and plum trees all blossom together at this time of the year.

Brimful of confidence I had walked ahead to the outskirts of the town, but once there I found I did not know which road to take for Takanagare. When I was a child I had only been there two or three times, so I wasn't really surprised that I had forgotten. And the area looked completely different from how I remembered it. I was perplexed.

"They've built a station and things, and now it has changed so much around here I no longer know how to get to Takanagare. I know it's that hill over there," I said, pointing to a light green hillock whose gentle slopes were visible ahead of us. "Let's hang around here for a while and wait for Aya and Yōko," I suggested cheerfully to Yōko's husband.

"Yes, why not." He was in good spirits too. "I hear the Aomori Prefecture Experimental Farm is somewhere around here." He knew more than I did.

"Is that so? Then let's go and look for it."

The experimental farm was on top of a low hill some fifty meters off the road and in to the right. It was built, it seems, to train new settlers and to produce farmers who could become village leaders, but its facilities are so splendid as to be almost a waste here in this wilderness in the far north. I hear that Prince Chichibu lent his enthusiastic support to this farm when he served with the Eighth Army Division in Hirosaki, and thanks to his patronage it now has an auditorium built in a grand style seldom seen in these parts, not to mention workshops, cattle sheds, fertilizer stores, and dormitories. Eyes wide open in wonder, I stood transfixed.

"Eh? I knew nothing at all about this! Isn't this far too good for Kanagi?" But even as I was speaking, I felt a strange, irrepressible joy. I may not wear my heart on my sleeve, but I am still a great fan of the place where I was born.

At the entrance to the farm stood a large commemorative stone, humble record of the following honors: in August 1935, a visit by Prince Asaka; in September of the same year, a visit by Prince Takamatsu; the following October, a visit by Prince and Princess Chichibu; in August 1938, a second visit by Prince Chichibu. The people of Kanagi should be much more proud of this farm: it is an everlasting source of pride not just for Kanagi, but for the whole Tsugaru Plain.

The vegetable patches, orchards, and rice fields—"practice plots" I believe they are called—planted by the model youths chosen from every farming community in Tsugaru, lay spread out quite beautifully behind the buildings. Yōko's husband walked around and gazed intently at the fields.

"This is great," he sighed. He's a landowner, so he must understand these things much better than someone like me.

"Look! Fuji! Splendid!" I cried out.

But it wasn't actually Mount Fuji. Where the view across the irrigated rice fields dissolved into the horizon, there was the gently floating figure of the Tsugaru Fuji—Mount Iwaki, 1,625 meters high. The mountain really did seem to be floating, unencumbered by weight. A lush deep green, it hovered silently in the blue sky, more feminine than Mount Fuji, its lower slopes like a gingko leaf standing on its wavy edge or like an ancient court dress folded open slightly, the symmetry of the folds exactly preserved. The mountain resembles a woman of an almost translucent grace and beauty. For all that, it's not very high.

"Well, Kanagi isn't a bad place at all," I mumbled in confusion. "Not bad at all." Grudgingly, the words came out.

"Nice, isn't it?" Yōko's husband said quietly.

During my trip I had the opportunity to observe the Tsugaru Fuji from various sides. Seen from Hirosaki, it is so massively imposing that it seems in a sense to belong to the town. On the other hand, I can never forget how classically graceful it looks from the center of the Tsugaru Plain. Seen from the coast, the mountain looks totally worthless—in tatters, no longer even the shadow of a beautiful woman. I have heard there is a tradition that in places from where Mount Iwaki can be seen at its best the rice ripens well and pretty girls abound. The rice is all right, I suppose, but even though the mountain looks particularly beautiful from northern Tsugaru, I could find precious little evidence of the pretty girls, although the weakness of my observational powers may be to blame for that.

"I wonder what happened to Aya and Yōko." I had suddenly begun to worry about them. "They must be far ahead of us by now."

We had been so absorbed in our admiration of the facilities of the experimental farm and the view that we had completely forgotten about the other two. We went back to the road and were looking all around, when Aya suddenly emerged from an inconspicuous little lane that branched off across the fields. He said with a smile that they had split up to look for us: Aya was searching the fields around here, and my niece had hurried along the road to Takanagare to catch up with us.

"Yōko was miserable without you, so I expect she'll have got quite far by now. Heeey!" he bawled in the direction she had taken, but there was no answer.

"Let's go." Aya swung the luggage onto his back. "This is the only road, so you don't have to worry about her."

In the sky the larks were singing away. It must have been some twenty years since I had last walked down the country lanes around my hometown in spring. Everywhere in the meadows there were shrubby thickets and little patches of marshy ground. The land undulated gently, and a decade ago people from the city would have praised it as the perfect golf course. But the cultivator's hoe is making steady inroads even in these wild fields; the roofs of the houses glitter in the sun; and as I listened to Aya's explanations about the infusion of life into the nearby hamlet and how that other cluster of houses belongs to the next village, I felt keenly that Kanagi had grown and gained in vitality.

Though we had gradually approached the beginning of the slope, there was still no sign of my niece.

"I wonder where she went." Like my mother, I worry about everything.

"Oh, she'll be around somewhere." The young husband kept his composure, ill at ease though he must have been.

"Anyway, let's ask someone." I doffed my rayon cap and greeted a farmer who was working in a field beside the road. "Did you by any chance see a young lady pass by?" I inquired. "She's dressed in Western clothes."

The answer was yes. Yes, she had passed by in such a hurry she was almost running. In my mind's eye I saw my niece scurrying down this lane decked with the colors of spring to catch up with her bridegroom, and I thought it wasn't a bad picture. After we had walked a little way up the hill, we saw her standing by the road in the shade of a larch, a smile on her face. When she had run this far and still not caught up with us, she had decided we must be behind her, so here she was gathering bracken. She didn't seem at all tired after her run.

The area around here, it seems, is a treasure-trove of wild vegetables such as bracken, spikenard, thistles, and bamboo shoots. In the autumn, *hatsutake*, peppercaps, *nameko*, and other mushrooms cover the ground "like a carpet," as Aya put it, and he told me that people come all the way from Goshogawara and Kizukuri to pick them.

"Miss Yōko is quite an expert at picking mushrooms," he added.

We were on our way up the hill again.

"I read that several members of the imperial family have visited Kanagi," I said to Aya.

"Yes," he answered with due decorum.

"Something to be grateful for."

"Yes." He was very formal.

"It's quite a privilege for a place like Kanagi that they should honor it with their presence."

"Yes."

"Did they come by car?"

"Yes, they came by car."

"And you too paid your respects, Aya?"

"Yes, I was granted that privilege."

"You're a happy man, then, Aya."

"Yes," he answered, wiping the sweat off his face with the towel he had wrapped around his neck.

The bush warblers were busily singing. Violets, dandelions, chrysanthemums, azaleas, white deutzias, akebis, roses, and all sorts of flowers whose names I did not know bloomed brightly in the grass on either side of our mountain path. The small willows and the oaks were in bud, and as we climbed further up the hill we saw vast stretches of bamboo grass. This hill is only some two hundred meters high, but it commands a fine view; one feels that from here one can see the whole of the Tsugaru Plain, from one end to the other. We would stop and look out over the plain and listen to Aya's explanations, then walk on a little further, and stop and look again to praise the view of the Tsugaru Fuji, and before we knew it we had arrived at the top.

"Is this the top?" I asked Aya, a trace of disappointment in my voice.

"Yes, this is it."

"Is this all?" I said, but then the sight of the Tsugaru Plain in spring, spread out before my eyes, took my breath away. The

Iwaki River was visible as a thin silver thread that sparkled in the sunlight. And that dull sheen, as of an ancient mirror, where the silver thread lost itself on the horizon, that must be Tappi Pond. And that white expanse appearing like hazy smoke far off in the distance must be Lake Jūsan, Lake Thirteen.

About Lake Jūsan, or Jūsan Lagoon, as it is also called, we read in "An Account of Jūsan": "Tsugaru has about thirteen rivers of varying lengths, all of which debouch here to form a large lake without any of them losing its own particular color." Situated in the north of the Tsugaru Plain, it is formed by the confluence of the Iwaki River and twelve other streams, big and small. Its circumference is about thirty kilometers, but because of the deposit the rivers carry with them it is shallow, about three meters at its deepest point, I am told. Since it is connected with the sea its water is salty, but since some water does enter the lake from the Iwaki River there is fresh water around the Iwaki estuary, and they say the lake contains both fresh-water and salt-water fish. On the south side of the channel that links the lake to the Japan Sea lies the small village of Jūsan. It is said that some seven or eight hundred years ago it was the headquarters of the dominant Tsugaru family, the Andō, and that during the Edo period both Jūsan and the port of Kodomari further to the north waxed exceedingly rich as loading ports for Tsugaru lumber and rice, but now there is not even a trace, not a memory of those days.

North of Lake Jūsan I could see Cape Gongen, but beyond it lies an area of vital importance for our national defense. We turn our eyes away, therefore, and gaze instead at a line far beyond the Iwaki River, a line clearly marked in an invigorating bluish green: the coast of the Japan Sea. We have an unobstructed view of Shichiri Nagahama, the Seven-League Strand. From Cape Gongen in the north to Cape Ōdose in the south there is nothing to interrupt the compass of our gaze.

"How beautiful! If it were up to me, I would build a castle

here," I said, but when Yōko wanted to know what I would do in winter, I was stuck for an answer.

"If only there were no snow. . . ," I sighed, feeling vaguely gloomy.

We went down to a mountain brook on the other side of the hill and opened our lunch boxes. Cooled in the brook, the beer was quite passable. My niece and Aya drank apple juice. It was just then that I spotted it.

"A snake!"

Yōko's husband grabbed his coat, which he had thrown on the ground, and jumped up.

"It's all right, don't worry," I said, pointing at the wall of rock that formed the opposite bank of the stream. "It's trying to climb up that rock wall."

It darted its head out of the whirling waters of the brook, rapidly scaled a few centimeters, and then fell back. Again it slithered up, and again it fell back. Tenaciously it tried some twenty times, and then I suppose it grew tired and gave up. It stretched out its body on the surface of the water and let the stream carry it where it would, until it started approaching our bank. Aya stood up. He grabbed a branch longer than he was, rushed off without a word, plunged into the brook, and lunged at the snake. We looked the other way.

"Is it dead? Is it dead?" my voice came out in tremulous tones.

"That tidies the place up." Aya tossed his branch into the stream, where it joined the snake.

"It wasn't a viper, was it?" His assurance had failed to dispel my fears.

"If it had been a viper, I'd have caught it alive, but this was only a 'green general.' The raw liver of a viper makes good medicine."

"Are there vipers in these hills?"

"Yes."

Glumly I returned to my beer.

Aya finished his lunch before the rest of us. He dragged over a huge log, threw it into the stream for a foothold, and nimbly hopped to the other side. He clambered up the rock wall and seemed to be gathering spikenard, thistles, and other wild vegetables.

"Watch out! Why do you have to look in such dangerous places? There are plenty elsewhere!" Trembling, I scolded Aya for the risks he was taking. "If you ask me, he just chose those dangerous spots to show how brave he is. I suppose he gets a kick out of it."

"Yes! Right!" my niece laughed loudly.

"Ayaaaa!" I bellowed. "That's enough. It's too dangerous—stop it!"

"O.K.," he answered, and climbed effortlessly down to safety. I sighed with relief.

On the way home, Yōko carried Aya's vegetables on her back—she was never one to worry much about her dress or appearance. The hiker who in Sotogahama had boasted that he was still young was tired now and had become remarkably quiet. As we were on our way down the hill, we heard the call of a cuckoo. At a sawmill just outside the town lay huge piles of logs, and there was a nonstop procession of trucks going in and out. It was the very picture of an affluent town.

"I can't believe how lively Kanagi has become," I said, to no one in particular.

"Do you think so?" My niece's husband seemed a little tired too. He sounded listless.

I suddenly felt embarrassed.

"I should mind my own business, I know, but you see, ten years ago Kanagi wasn't like this. Then it looked like a town that was gradually dying. Now it feels as if it has somehow come back to life."

When we got home, I told my brother that the scenery around

Kanagi was rather pleasant and that I had revised my opinion of it, and he answered that as you get older, you begin to wonder whether the scenery of the place where you were born and raised is not superior to that of Kyoto and Nara.

The next day my brother and his wife joined the party of the previous day on an expedition to the Kanoko River reservoir, about six kilometers southeast of Kanagi. Just as we were about to leave, some people came to see my brother, so we went ahead without him. My sister-in-law wore baggy pants, white socks, and straw sandals. This was perhaps the longest walk she had taken since coming to Kanagi as a bride.

That day too the weather was fine, even hotter than the day before. Guided by Aya, we tramped along the tracks of the forest railroad, which followed the course of the Kanagi River. The ties were laid too close together for a whole step, but too far apart for half a step—an extremely malicious arrangement that made it very awkward to walk. I got tired, quickly fell silent, and was constantly wiping the sweat off my face. It seems that when the weather is too beautiful, travelers just get dog-tired, and their spirits droop rather than soar.

"Around here you can see the traces of the big flood," Aya had stopped to explain. Giant roots, stumps, and logs lay scattered over several hectares of paddy and vegetable fields near the river, giving it the appearance of a field after a violent battle. The year before, such a devastating flood had hit Kanagi that even my grandmother said she had never experienced anything like it in all her eighty-eight years.

"These trees were washed down from the mountains." A look of sadness clouded Aya's face.

"How awful." I wiped the sweat off my brow. "It must have looked just like the sea."

"It did."

We left the Kanagi River and for a while followed the Kanoko

River upstream. At long last we were rid of the railroad tracks. We´ made a slight turn to the right and came upon a large reservoir—I would say about two kilometers in circumference—brimming over with deep-blue water. "When a lone bird breaks into song, the hills sound even stiller." These words seemed to have been written for this place.

I am told this used to be a deep ravine known as the Sōzaemon Gorge, but a dam was built across the Kanoko River, which flowed through the gorge, and this big reservoir was the result. That was in 1941, really very recently. The large stone marker on its bank has, among other names, that of my brother chiseled on it.

Because the red cliffs around the reservoir still bore the fresh scars of the construction work, the scenery lacked what one might call natural majesty, but I could feel the strength of the community of Kanagi and sensed that this creation of human hands would ultimately mature into a delightful landscape. Such were the inspired thoughts that occurred to the astute traveling critic as he stood there, puffing at his cigarette and staring about him this way and that.

I strode on confidently and led our little party along the bank of the reservoir.

"It's beautiful here, really beautiful," I said, as I sat down in the shade of a tree on a little promontory. "Aya, do me a favor, will you, and check whether this is a lacquer tree." It would have been too awful for words if I had had to continue my trip with lacquer poisoning.

It was not a lacquer tree, he told me.

"Yes, but how about that tree over there? It looks suspicious. Check it for me, would you?" Everyone laughed, but I was serious.

It wasn't a lacquer tree either. Completely reassured, I decided this would be a good spot to open our lunch boxes.

A couple of beers put me in the right mood for a yarn. I

told them about the excitement I had felt when I first saw the sea. It was during a school excursion to Takayama, a high dune on the west coast, about fourteen kilometers from Kanagi, and I must have been in the second or third grade of elementary school. The teacher in charge was the most excited of all: he made us stand in two lines facing the sea and sing "I Am a Child of the Sea." On this, the first occasion that I saw the sea in my life, to sing this song of children born on the coast, with lines that go "I am a child of the sea/ Of the pine grove on the shore /Where the white waves sing their song," struck me as thoroughly unnatural, and it embarrassed and bothered me, child though I was.

I had spent a great deal of care on my attire for the excursion: a broad-brimmed straw hat, a stick of plain wood that my eldest brother had used to climb Mount Fuji and whose attraction lay in the marks of the Fuji shrines branded all over it, and although the teacher had told us to dress as lightly as we could and to wear straw sandals, I alone wore a useless formal skirt, long socks, and high, laced shoes. Prettily dolled up in this way I set off, but before I had walked two kilometers I was worn out. First they made me take off my skirt and shoes. Then I was given straw sandals—a wretched, threadbare, odd pair, one with a loop of red cloth, the other with a loop of straw. In due time my hat was taken off, my stick confiscated, and at long last they made me climb onto the cart which they used at school to carry the sick. When I came home, holding my shoes in one hand and leaning on my stick with the other, my appearance had lost every trace of the luster with which it had glittered when I left that morning.

I had pulled out all the stops, and everybody was in stitches.

"Halloooo!" someone was calling. It was my brother.

"Halloooo!" we shouted back in unison and Aya ran off to meet him.

Soon my brother appeared, alpenstock in hand. I had drunk the last drop of beer and now felt extremely guilty. He ate his lunch straightaway, and then we all walked to the far side of the reservoir. Suddenly we heard a loud rustling noise: a water bird took off from the pond. Yōko's husband and I looked at each other and nodded inanely. Neither of us seemed to have the courage to inquire whether it was a goose or a duck. At any rate, it was definitely a wild water bird, and its flight drew us under the spell of the deep mountain folds.

My brother walked silently, his back stooped. How many years had it been since I last went walking with him? About ten years ago we had walked down a rural lane in a Tokyo suburb, my brother silent and his back stooped, like now, and I a few paces behind him, looking at his back and sobbing. This was surely the first time since then. I doubt that my brother has ever forgiven me for that incident.[7] Perhaps he never will, as long as he lives. A broken cup cannot be mended. No matter what you do, it will never be as before. The people of Tsugaru, even more than others, are a race of people who do not forget when their feelings have been hurt. I had thought at the time that I might never have another chance to go walking with my brother.

Gradually the sound of falling water grew louder. At the far end of the reservoir is one of the best-known sites in these parts, the Kanoko Falls. Before long, the waterfall came into view below us. It was narrow and barely fifteen or so meters high. We were walking up a mere strip of a path, just wide enough for one person, that ran alongside Sōzaemon Gorge, the mountain rising sheer like a screen to our right, and on our left a steep cliff starting at our feet. At the bottom of the ravine, the pool below the waterfall was a deep, deep green.

"Oh dear, I do feel dizzy!" my sister-in-law said, only half joking. She grasped Yōko's hand and walked as if she were quite frightened.

To our right, on the mountainside, the azaleas were ablaze with color. My brother had swung his alpenstock over his shoulder, and every time we came to a spot where they bloomed in full glory, he would slow down. The wisterias, too, had begun to blossom.

By and by the path turned downhill again, and we descended to the top of the waterfall. In the middle of the little brook, not much wider than a door, someone had laid the stump of a tree, and with that as a foothold we were able to make it across the stream in two steps. One after another we hopped across. My sister-in-law alone stayed behind.

"I can't!" All she could do was laugh; she wouldn't even try. Her feet seemed frozen and unable to move forward.

"Carry her on your back," my brother said to Aya, but even with Aya at her side she just laughed and waved her hands impotently. Then Aya, in a display of superhuman strength, grabbed hold of an enormous tree trunk and launched it into the stream just above the top of the waterfall. Now they had a bridge of sorts. My sister-in-law tried to cross, but it seemed her legs simply refused to perform. Holding Aya by the shoulders, she finally made it as far as the middle, and because the rest of the brook was shallow, she jumped from the improvised bridge and splashed through the stream over to our bank. The hem of her pants, her white socks, and her sandals were soaking wet.

"I look as if I've just come back from Takayama," she laughed, suddenly recalling my story about the sorry figure I had cut when I returned from my excursion. Yōko and her husband burst into laughter, but my brother looked back over his shoulder.

"Eh? What?"

Everyone stopped laughing. He looked puzzled, so I thought about explaining the joke to him, but the story was really too silly, and I didn't have the nerve to explain the origin of "the way back from Takayama" all over again.

Without a word, my brother walked on. He is always left out.

1 (p. 103)   Mutsushū is a shorter reading of Michi-no-oku-shū (*shū* meaning "province"), and because the character *oku* (奥) has the alternative reading *ō*, Ōshū developed as an alternative for Mutsushū. The name Ōu (奥羽) is a combination of the characters *ō* of Ōshū and *wa* (羽) of Dewa, here pronounced in its alternative reading *u*. Uninitiated readers will be forgiven for not being able to follow this argument immediately.

2 (p. 105)   *Abe no Yoritoki.* The tale to which Professor Ogawa refers relates how Abe no Yoritoki, one of the principal characters of the Earlier Nine Years' War (see Appendix II), flees from Japan to escape from Minamoto no Yoriyoshi, but finds no shelter across the sea and returns to Mutsu. The country he visits is described as "across the sea from the Ezo territory in deep Mutsu" (i.e. Akita and Tsugaru) and would seem to be identical with the territory formerly occupied by the Korean kingdom of Parhae.

3 (p. 105)   *Taiwanese aborigines.* This may be a reference to the expedition led by Saigō Tsugumichi in 1874, which was sent to punish the Taiwanese for having killed a number of Japanese fishermen.

4 (p. 118)   *"When a lone bird . . ."* A line from a poem by the Chinese philosopher-statesman Wang An-shih (1012–86).

5 (p. 118)   *Enomoto Kikaku.* Also known as Takari Kikaku (1661–1707), a disciple of Bashō. According to Kagami Shikō, another disciple, Bashō first wrote the second and third lines of this haiku, and Kikaku suggested "yellow roses" as the first line. Bashō, however, decided in favor of "an old pond." For an account and discussion, see Donald Keene, *World Within Walls* (Tokyo: Tuttle, 1978), pp. 88–90.

6 (p. 118)   *"Come with me . . ."* A haiku by Kobayashi Issa (1768–1827), one of the great masters of the genre, who is said to have written this poem at the age of five, after the death of his mother.

7 (p. 131)   *That incident.* It is not clear exactly which incident Dazai has in mind here. His brother Bunji traveled down to Tokyo on several occasions to solve Dazai's problems, which varied from attempted suicide to left-wing activities.

V

The West Coast

I have mentioned several times before that although I was born and brought up here, until now I knew next to nothing about Tsugaru. I had never again visited its Japan Sea coast since that excursion to Takayama in my second or third year at elementary school. Takayama, a hill on the coast some fourteen kilometers west of Kanagi, stands just outside Shariki, a fairly large village of about five thousand people. The Takayama Inari Shrine is said to be famous. However, we are discussing my boyhood memories, and the only thing I can still remember vividly is my blunder over the clothes; all the rest has become a vague blur.

From the beginning I had planned to avail myself of this opportunity to travel the length of Tsugaru's west coast. And so the day after our outing to the Kanoko reservoir I left Kanagi for Goshogawara. I changed to a train on the Goshogawara-Noshiro line at about eleven in the morning, and ten minutes can hardly have passed before I arrived in Kizukuri, where I thought I should take a brief look around. On leaving the station, I found myself in a timeworn and tranquil town. Kizukuri has just slightly over four thousand inhabitants, so it is smaller than Kanagi, though it seems older. I could vaguely hear the rumbling of the machines of a rice refinery. Somewhere under the eaves of a house a pigeon was cooing.

My father was born here. For several generations the Tsushima family in Kanagi had only produced daughters and had therefore had to adopt successive sons-in-law to continue the family name. My father was the third son of the M. family, of old Kizukuri stock, but he married into the Tsushima family of Kanagi, took their name, and so became the next head of that family. He died when I was fourteen, so I cannot say that I knew what sort of person he really was. Let me quote again from "Memories":

Because my father was a very busy man, he was seldom at home, and even when he was, he did not spend time with his children. I was afraid of him. On one occasion I wanted his fountain pen, but could not bring myself to say so outright; I fretted and fretted over it, and then, one night as I lay in bed, eyes closed and pretending to be talking in my sleep, I called out softly to my father, who was in the next room in conversation with some guests: "Fountain pen . . . fountain pen. . . ." But of course my words reached neither his ears nor his heart.

And on another occasion, when my younger brother and I had got into the granary, which was cram-full of rice bags, and were playing some interesting game, my father suddenly appeared at the door and shouted: "Out, you rascals! Out!" He was blocking the light; his big frame appeared pitch-black. It still gives me the shivers to think of the terror I felt at that moment. . . .

The next spring, while the snow was still deep, my father vomited blood and died in a Tokyo hospital. A local paper carried the news of his death in an extra edition. This fact impressed me more than my father's death. My name also appeared in the paper as one of the bereaved relatives.

My father's remains were put into a big coffin and taken home on a sledge. With a whole crowd of townspeople I went almost to the next village to meet it. When the sledges at last came gliding in procession out of the shade of the forest, I was struck by the beauty of the moonlight shining on the sledge hoods. The next day the relatives and family servants gathered in the room containing the family altar, where my father's coffin had been placed. When the lid was removed, everyone began to weep loudly. It was as if my father was sleeping. The high bridge of his nose had turned pale. When I heard everyone sobbing, it brought tears to my eyes as well.

These are the sort of things I remember about my father. After he died, I transferred the awe I had felt for him to my eldest brother. This gave me a sense of security, of support; not once did I feel sad because I no longer had a father. However, as I get older, I find myself wondering—rather discourteously—what on earth my father was really like, and when I doze off in my Tokyo hovel, he sometimes appears in my dreams. He did not really die, but had to go into hiding for some political reason; he is a little older and more tired than I remember him, and it fills me with a terrible longing for him. A silly dream, I'm afraid. But it is true that recently my interest in my father has grown tremendously.

My father's brothers and sisters all had weak lungs, and although he did not die of pulmonary tuberculosis, he did after all throw up blood and die because of some problem with his respiratory organs. He was fifty-three when he died, which to my child's eyes seemed frightfully old. I thought at first he had died of old age. Now I no longer think of death at the age of fifty-three as a peaceful passing away after many years of physical decline, but as terribly premature. I sometimes entertain the conceited idea that if my father could have been spared a little longer, he might have been of much, much greater service to Tsugaru. Now I wanted to see in what kind of house he was born and in what kind of town he grew up.

Kizukuri consists of just two rows of houses on either side of a single road. Behind the houses lie beautifully plowed rice fields, with here and there a row of poplar trees. I had never seen poplars in Tsugaru before. I have seen many elsewhere, to be sure, but I do not remember them so vividly as I now do those poplars of Kizukuri, their young, light green leaves trembling enchantingly in the soft breeze. Seen from here, the Tsugaru Fuji looks just as it does from Kanagi: an elegant and very beautiful woman. And as for the story that in places from which the mountain looks beautiful, the rice and the women also grow up beautifully—the rice around here certainly seems plentiful, but I'm not sure the same can be said of beautiful women. As in Kanagi, things looked if anything rather discouraging. On this point I was tempted to think that reality might be the opposite of what the story claims: in places from which Mount Iwaki looks beautiful . . . But no, I don't think I ought to say this. It would give great offense. A mere passer-by who has walked around town but once hardly has a right to jump to this sort of conclusion.

The weather was again inexpressibly fine. A trace of spring mist hung hazily over the straight concrete road that led away from the station. Basking in the spring sun, I strolled down the street, my rubber soles making less noise that a cat's paws. The weather must have affected my thinking: when I saw the sign "Kizukuri Police Station," I read it as "wooden police station."[1]

"Of course," I nodded knowingly, "it's a wooden building." But then I did a double take and smiled wryly at my mistake.

Kizukuri still has *komohi*. In the old days all the stores on the Ginza, without exception, let down awnings over their shop fronts when the afternoon sun shone too brightly, and you, my dear reader, would walk underneath the awnings out of the heat of the sun. It would probably feel just as if you were walking down a long, improvised passageway. Well, if you think of the *komohi* of the north country as long passageways formed not by awnings but by permanent solid structures—the eaves of houses extended a little way forward—you will have a fairly accurate picture. They are not, mind you, built as protection against the sun—nothing as fancy as that. The eaves of the houses are joined together so that in winter, when the snow piles up high, it is easy to get from one house to the next. In blizzards, for instance, there is no fear of being exposed to the elements, and under more normal conditions one can go shopping without having to worry about the weather. They are, therefore, a great convenience. They also make a safer place for children to play than the sidewalks of Tokyo. On rainy days these long passageways make life much easier for pedestrians, and to travelers like me, who seek shelter from the spring heat, they are deliciously cool. While it is true that one is exposed to the minor inconvenience of being stared at by the people working in the shops, they are nonetheless something to be grateful for.

It is generally believed that the word *komohi* is a dialect version of *komise*, small store, but it amuses me to think that a derivation from *komose*, enclosed current, or *komohi*, confined sunlight, is probably much easier to understand. The *komohi* in this town are very long. It seems that most older Tsugaru towns have them, but there can be few places so completely dominated by them as Kizukuri. It is a regular *komohi* town.

Walking down the passageway, I arrived at the M. Pharmaceutical Wholesale Company. This is the house where my father was born. I passed straight by without even stopping, pondering my next move. I walked on for a while until I reached the end of the passageways, and then, with a sigh, turned around and retraced my steps. Until then I had never visited the M. family house. I had never even been to Kizukuri unless, perhaps, someone took me there when I was very young. At any rate, I don't remember such visits. The present head of the M. family is a merry soul, some four or five years older than I am. He has often been to our house in Kanagi, so it's not as if we were complete strangers. If I visited him now he would of course not look displeased, but still, everything considered, my dropping in would be rather sudden. Imagine the scene: here I am, in this bedraggled outfit, greeting Mr. M. with an obsequious smile on my face and nothing special to talk about. Would he not be startled and think that I had at last found it impossible to make a living in Tokyo and had come to borrow money or something? On the other hand, it would sound awfully affected if I told him that before I died I wanted to see the house where my father was born. These are not words that a man in the prime of his life can easily get past his lips.

While I was still considering whether or not I should simply go back to the station, I had again reached the M. store. I would probably never have this opportunity again. I would just have to grin and bear it. Let's go in.

I made up my mind on the spot and called out toward the back of the store, "Is anybody home?"

Mr. M. appeared.

"Well, well, well! Look who's here!"

He gave me no chance to say anything, but pulled me straight into the parlor and forced me down in the seat of honor in front of the alcove.

"Fancy that! . . . Sake!" he ordered, and within two or three minutes the sake appeared. What speed!

"It's been a long time! A long time!" Mr. M. helped himself to some hefty gulps of sake. "How long has it been since you last came to Kizukuri?"

"Well, assuming I came here as a child, some thirty years, I'd say."

"So it must be. Come on, drink up! When you come to Kizukuri you don't behave like a stranger. But I'm glad you came. Really, I'm glad."

The floor plan of the house looked very much like that of our house in Kanagi. I had heard how, soon after he had been adopted into the family, my father had built a completely new house of his own design in Kanagi. But that was not true at all. On coming to Kanagi, he had simply built the house to resemble his home in Kizukuri. It made me glow with happiness when I realized I understood what my father, the adopted bridegroom, must have felt. Then it occurred to me that the arrangement of the trees and stones in the garden was also very similar. Even though it was a trifling thing I had discovered, I felt I had come closer to my dead father, and this was a result of my unpremeditated visit to Mr. M.'s house.

Mr. M. was about to fill my cup again.

"No, thank you, I've had enough. I've got to catch the one o'clock train for Fukaura."

"Fukaura? What for?"

"No special reason. I just want to see what it looks like."

"Are you going to write about it?"

"Yes, I guess so. . . ." I couldn't very well dampen his spirits with my intimations of mortality.

"Then you'll also be writing about Kizukuri. And if you do," Mr. M. was making no bones about it, "I want you to be sure to emphasize how much rice we deliver to the government. If you compare all the police districts in the country, the Kizukuri district delivers the most. Top in Japan! And how do we do it? . . . We break our backs—I think I can safely say that. When all the fields around here were suffering from a water shortage, I went and got water from the next village, and the results were

140

fantastic. I used to be known as the bottomless well, but now they all call me the magic fountain. We landowners can't just sit here and twiddle our thumbs! I have a bad back, but I still went to weed the rice fields. Yes, we'll see to it that you people in Tokyo get a lot of fine rice rationed out to you this time.''

You can take him at his word. Mr. M. has always been a generous person, ever since he was a child. With his winning, childlike, big round eyes, he enjoys the respect and affection of everyone here. I offered a silent prayer for his happiness and, barely managing to ward off his invitations to stay, I took my leave and was just in time for the 1:00 P.M. train for Fukaura.

Within some thirty minutes the train had taken me from Kizukuri along the Goshogawara-Noshiro line through Narusawa and Ajigasawa. The Tsugaru Plain had already come to an end, and from here on the train ran along the Japan Sea coast. For the next hour or so I looked out at the sea on the right and the foothills of the northern part of the Dewa range immediately to the left, and then beautiful Cape Ōdose came into view through the window to the right.

The rocks here are all said to be breccia—angular stones and rocks cemented with volcanic ashes. At the end of the Edo period a section of the speckled green bedrock, leveled through marine erosion, rose to the surface as if by magic, and because it forms a floor on which several hundred people could hold a banquet, this part of the shore was given the name Senjōjiki, the Thousand-Tatami Floor. Here and there in the rocks are round hollows that fill up with sea water and resemble large cups overflowing with *sake*, and this is why—so I am told—the rocks are also called Sakazuki Numa, the *Sake*-Cup Swamp. The person who first saw a resemblance between *sake* cups and those large holes, which range in width from about thirty centimeters to twice that size, must have been quite a drinker.

''On the shore stand fantastically eroded crags, their feet incessantly washed by the billows." Now that's what I would write if I employed the style of the tourist guides. However, the coastline here does not possess that uncanny, forbidding quality of northern Sotogahama. It has become, so to speak, the kind of ordinary "scenery" you can see all over the country; it does not breathe that peculiar Tsugaru atmosphere, which, like a difficult handwriting, is all but unintelligible to strangers. It is, in a word, civilized. It has been caressed by human eyes, and become soft and domesticated.

Takeuchi Unpei writes in his *History of Aomori Prefecture* that the region south of here used to be part of the Akita domain and not of Tsugaru, but he adds that there are records stating that in 1603 the region was joined to Tsugaru after negotiations with the Satake family, who ruled the neighboring domain. I myself have nothing to go on but the unreliable intuition of a traveling vagabond, but I can't help feeling that this area is not really Tsugaru. There is nothing here of Tsugaru's luckless karma; the clumsy tactlessness so typical of Tsugaru is absent. Just looking at the landscape, you can sense it—it is knowing, cultured, as it were. Its heart contains no mulish pride.

Some forty minutes after Ōdose the train arrives at Fukaura. This port greets its visitors with the same kind of silence one often encounters in the fishing villages on the Chiba coast: a modest and gentle attitude that suggests no one would ever pry into your private affairs—or if you want to put it less flatteringly, there is a shrewd and calculating feeling to the town. In short, Fukaura shows a complete indifference toward visitors.

Far be it from me to reproach a town for its atmosphere. I wonder that people can carry on living in this world without that sort of approach. Is this not the attitude of people who have grown up, who have reached adulthood? Deep down, they have confidence in themselves. Like children who do not know when they are beaten, the people of the northern part of Tsugaru struggle against the odds, but you will find no such battles here. Northern Tsugaru is like a half-cooked vegetable, but this region has been cooked to the point of transparency. Yes, that's it—compare the two that way and it's easier to understand. The people of the Tsugaru heartland really lack confidence in their own history. They haven't a trace of it. That's why they end up assuming that posture of arrogance, why they square their shoulders and accuse others of being "base." It's the basis of the obstinacy, the stubbornness, and the complexity of the Tsugaru people, and ultimately the cause of their sad destiny of isolation and loneliness.

People of Tsugaru! Raise your heads and take courage! Didn't someone once feel compelled to say that Tsugaru is imbued with the same pent-up energy that existed in Italy immediately before the Renaissance? Consider quietly one night, I ask you, to what extent the great, the unfulfilled promise of Tsugaru can be a source of hope for the nation when its spiritual and cultural development has reached a dead end. But you just square your shoulders in that unnatural way of yours. No one can give you self-confidence but you yourselves. Without bothering about others, but with confidence in ourselves, let's not give up the good fight yet.

The town of Fukaura, which now has a population of about five thousand, used to be the southernmost harbor on the west coast of the old Tsugaru domain. During the Edo period it fell under the jurisdiction of the Warden of the Four Ports—together with Aomori, Ajigasawa, and Jūsan. It was, therefore, one of the most important harbors of the domain. It lies on a small bay surrounded by hills, and is known for the deep, calm waters of its harbor, for the weirdly shaped rocks of Azuma Beach, for its Benten Island, and for Cape Yukiai. This is the sum of the scenic spots on the coast. Fukaura is a quiet town. In the gardens of the fishermen's houses, fine, big diving suits are hung upside down to dry. There is a feeling of resignation in the air, a tranquillity that borders on stagnation. Straight down the road from the station stands a temple—Enkakuji. It has an impressive gate, guarded by the two protective deities, and its Yakushi Hall has now been designated a National Treasure.

I visited the temple, and then thought it was about time to leave Fukaura. These perfectly finished towns make a traveler feel lonely. I went to the beach, sat down on a rock, and tried to make up my mind what to do next. It was still early. I suddenly thought of my little girl, back home in Tokyo. I do my best not to think of her, but sometimes when I feel empty her image comes floating into my mind and makes me feel emptier still. I got up, went to the post office to buy a postcard, and wrote a line or two to my abandoned family. My daughter was suffering from whooping cough, and my wife was expecting our second child sometime soon. Overwhelmed by an almost unbearable desire to be with them, I entered the first inn I saw and was shown to a dirty room, where I ordered *sake* before I had undone my puttees. They soon brought the *sake*, plus a tray with food. The service was unexpectedly quick, and that cheered me up a bit. The room was dirty, but the tray was loaded with sea bream and abalone—which seem to be the main products of this port— prepared in various ways. I drank the two flasks of *sake*, but it was still too early to turn in.

Since the start of my journey, I had always been treated by others, but suddenly the unedifying thought occurred to me that tonight for once I might try to get drunk all by myself. In the corridor I found the girl who had brought me my tray and asked her (she was only about twelve) whether there was any more *sake*, but the answer was no. But when I asked her if there was any other place I could get a drink, she promptly answered yes. Much relieved, I asked where, and on following her directions came upon an unexpectedly cozy little restaurant. I was shown up to a ten-mat room on the second floor overlooking the sea and sat down comfortably at a Tsugaru lacquer table.

"*Sake, sake,*" I ordered, and at once they brought *sake*, and nothing else. That was really nice. Usually they take their time preparing food and keep their customers waiting, but my order was served straightaway, by a waitress in her forties whose front teeth were missing. I thought she might be the right person to tell me a little about the local traditions.

"What are the famous sites here in Fukaura?"

"Have you been to the Kannon Temple?"

"The Kannon Temple? Ah, now that would be another name for Enkakuji, right? Yes, I've been there."

I was just thinking this waitress might be able to tell me some old stories when a pudgy, somewhat younger maid showed up, cracking all sorts of silly jokes. She got on my nerves so much that, in my conviction that a man should at all times be frank, I simply had to say to her:

"Excuse me, but would you mind going downstairs?"

Reader, I warn you. When a man enters a restaurant, he must never speak frankly. I had really put my foot in my mouth. The young maid got up in a huff, the older waitress departed with her, and I was left completely alone. If you send one out of the room, it seems to be irreconcilable with the code of comradely conduct for the other to remain seated without protest. I drank my *sake* all by myself in that big room, gazed at the light of the Fukaura lighthouse, and felt the loneliness of the traveler more deeply than ever. I returned to my lodgings.

The next morning I was eating breakfast, still feeling lonely, when the landlord brought up a small tray with a flask of *sake*.

"Excuse me, but aren't you Mr. Tsushima?" he asked.

"Yes, I am."

I had registered under my pen name, Dazai.

"I thought so. I thought you looked like him. I'm a classmate of your brother Eiji; we went to middle school together. You registered as Mr. Dazai and so I didn't realize who you were, but you look so much like him. . . ."

"Still, it's not a false name."

"Yes, yes, I know. I had heard there was a younger brother who wrote fiction under another name. I'm really sorry I didn't welcome you personally last night. Won't you accept this *sake*? And here on the tray there's some salted abalone entrails. They go really well with *sake*."

I finished my breakfast and then enjoyed the *sake*, and the salted entrails. They were delicious. Really good. So my brothers stood me in good stead even in this far corner of Tsugaru. I realized that after all I could not do a single thing by myself, and this made the delicate taste of the entrails even more memorable. In brief, the only thing I had learned in this port on the southern border of the Tsugaru domain was the extent of my brothers' influence. A bit dazed by the discovery I got on the train.

Ajigasawa. On my way back from Fukaura I stopped off in this old port town. Ajigasawa was Tsugaru's central west coast port and it seems to have been very prosperous during the Edo period. The rice grown in Tsugaru was loaded and shipped from here, and it was a port of call for Osaka-bound vessels. It was also a thriving fishing town, and the fish hauled in along its shore graced the tables not only of the houses of the domain's capital, but also of every part of the wide Tsugaru Plain. However, today it has a population of only about forty-five hundred, making it smaller than Kizukuri or Fukaura, and the vigor and strength it possessed in former days seem to be on the wane.

With a name like Ajigasawa, Horse Mackerel Depths, you would expect that at some time in the past they caught shoals of fine horse mackerel here, but even when we were kids we never heard a thing about them. Only its sandfish are famous. Once in a while these sandfish are rationed out in Tokyo too, so perhaps my readers have come across them. They are little fish without scales, fifteen to twenty centimeters long, and reminiscent of sea smelt. A specialty of the west coast, they are caught in large numbers off Akita Prefecture. People from Tokyo might consider them unpleasantly oily, but to us their taste seems extremely delicate. In Tsugaru the first sandfish of the season are boiled whole in a thin soy sauce and eaten one after the other, and people who put away twenty or thirty without batting an eye are by no means rare. I have often heard of sandfish clubs, with prizes for those who eat the largest number of fish. Since the sandfish that reach Tokyo are no longer fresh, and people don't know how to prepare them, I imagine they do taste awful. However, sandfish appear in haiku almanacs, and I remember I once read a reference to their light, pleasant taste in a haiku by an Edo-period poet, so it is possible that the sophisticates of Edo prized them as delicacies. Be that as it may, eating sandfish is without any doubt one of the great pleasures of the Tsugaru winter hearth.

Because of these sandfish I had been familiar with the name of Ajigasawa since my childhood, but this was the first time I had visited it. Hemmed in between the mountains and the sea, it's a frightful straggle of a town. It was pervaded by a strangely stagnant, sweet-and-sour smell that reminded me of Bonchō's haiku, "In the city / What a heavy smell of things . . ." The river water, too, is sluggish and muddy. The town is somehow tired. As in Kizukuri, there are long *komohi* passageways, but the ones here are beginning to show signs of wear and tear and are not as refreshingly cool as those of Kizukuri.

The day was again clear and beautiful, but, even though I walked down the passageways to escape the burning sun, I felt stifled in an odd sort of way. There are many restaurants, and one can imagine the "taverns" of old probably did a thriving trade around here. Even now the people in the row of four or five noodle shops were calling out to the passers-by, "Take a rest here!" which sounds strange in this day and age—like a relic of the past. As it was just about noon, I went into one of the shops. The noodles, with two plates of grilled fish, came to forty sen. And the soup in which the noodles were served wasn't at all bad.

However, that doesn't change the fact that Ajigasawa drags on. It really is nothing more than one street along the shore, one identical house after the other, without variation. I must have walked a few kilometers when at last I arrived at the outskirts of town and turned back. Ajigasawa has no center. In most towns the houses are clustered around some central point where even travelers just passing through without stopping can sense that they are in the heart of town. But in Ajigasawa there is nothing of the sort. It seemed to me to be dangling loose, like a folding fan with a broken pivot. The absence of a center was so depressing that I even wondered—shades of politics, à la Degas—whether Ajigasawa might not be in the grips of a power struggle, or some such trouble.

I am forced to smile as I write this, for if I had had a good friend in Fukaura or Ajigasawa who had met me at the station and told me how glad he was I could come and shown me around and explained things to me, then I would—naively—have ignored my intuition and written with an inspired pen what pure Tsugaru towns Fukaura and Ajigasawa are. Observations like the ones I have been making do not really belong in a record of traveling impressions. If anyone from Fukaura or Ajigasawa should happen to be reading this book, I hope he will smile and forgive me. This travelogue is simply too shallow to be able to tarnish his hometown.

Leaving Ajigasawa, I got back on the train and arrived in Goshogawara at two in the afternoon. From the station I went straight to Mr. Nakabata's house. I think I wrote enough about him in my two recent stories, "Going Home" and "My Hometown," so I will not repeat myself and bore you, but I owe him a great deal: he undertook—cheerfully—to save me from the dissolute life I was leading in my twenties.

It was painful to see how Mr. Nakabata had aged in the little time since I had seen him last. He told me that he had fallen ill the previous year and lost a lot of weight.

"Hard times, you know. So you came all the way from Tokyo dressed like this?"

Nevertheless, he looked glad as he subjected my beggarly appearance to a thorough inspection.

"Your socks have holes in them."

He got up himself, took a pair of socks out of a dresser, and pushed them in my direction.

"I was thinking of going on to Haikara-chō."

"Oh, good idea. Off you go then. Keiko, show him the way!"

No matter how much weight Mr. Nakabata had lost, he was still as impetuous as ever.

My aunt lives in Haikara-chō, the Smart Quarter. That's what it was called when I was young, but now the name has been changed to Ōmachi, the Large Quarter, or something like that. Goshogawara, which I have already mentioned in my Introduction, figures prominently among my childhood memories. Four or five years ago I published the following sketch in a Goshogawara paper:

> Because my aunt lives in Goshogawara, I often used to visit the town as a child. I was at the opening of the Asahi Theater, which must have been when I was in the third or fourth grade of elementary school. I am almost certain I saw To-mo'emon. His Ume no Yoshibei made me cry. That was the first time I ever saw a revolving stage, and I was so amazed I instinctively got to my feet. Soon afterward there was a fire at the Asahi Theater and it burned to the ground. We could clearly see the blaze in Kanagi. They said the fire had started in the projection room. About ten young schoolchildren who had come to watch a movie were killed.

The projectionist was held responsible. "Accidental bodily injury resulting in death," they called it. I do not know why, but even though I was only a child at the time, I have never been able to forget the name of the projectionist's offense nor the power of destiny. I have also heard people say that the theater burned down because of some relationship between the name Asahi and the word *hi*, fire. This happened some twenty years ago.

I must have been seven or eight years old, when, walking through Goshogawara's bustling streets, I fell into a ditch. It was fairly deep—about a meter perhaps. The water came almost to my chin. It was night. A man reached down from above, and I grabbed hold of his hand. I was hauled up and undressed in front of the staring crowd, which really upset me. We were right in front of a secondhand store, and they quickly covered me with some old clothes from the shop: a girl's summer kimono, with a green waistband as a makeshift sash. I felt terribly embarrassed. My aunt came running up to the store, her face ashen. I had always been her special pet. Because I was ugly, people were always making fun of me, and as a result I developed a grudge against the whole world. My aunt was the only one to call me handsome. When other people maligned my looks, she would become genuinely angry. All these things have become old memories.

I left Mr. Nakabata's house with Keiko, his only child.
"I'd like to see the Iwaki River. Is it far from here?"
She said it was quite near.
"Then will you take me?"
After Keiko had led me through the town for only about five minutes, we reached the river. My aunt used to take me there frequently when I was a child, but it had seemed much further

from town. For a child's feet this was a great distance. I was, moreover, the type of child who was always indoors and afraid to go out. When I did leave the house, I used to be so tense that the world would swim before my eyes, and this must have made the river seem all the farther off. There was the bridge, not so different from how I remembered it. Looking at it now, I still thought it was rather long.

"It's called Inui Bridge, isn't it?"

"Yes."

"Inui. I wonder how you write that. With the old character for 'northwest,' perhaps?"

"Could be," she laughed.

"Not very sure, are you! Oh well, it doesn't matter. Let's cross over."

I stroked the railing with one hand as we made our way slowly across the bridge. It was a nice view. Of the rivers in the suburbs of Tokyo, the outlet of the Arakawa looks most like it. The air shimmered in the green grass that grew all along the riverbed. It made one quite dizzy. The waters of the Iwaki River flowed by, lapping the grass on either bank and glittering brightly.

"In summer everybody comes here to enjoy the evening breeze. Not that they have anywhere else to go."

The people of Goshogawara like their fun, so I could imagine what a lively scene it would be.

"That's the memorial shrine for the war dead over there. They've just finished it," Keiko told me, pointing upstream. "The shrine Daddy's so proud of," she added softly, with a smile.

It seemed to be a splendid building. Mr. Nakabata is on the board of the veterans' organization. No doubt he demonstrated that gallant spirit of his when it came to the work on the shrine.

We had crossed over and stopped at the foot of the bridge to talk a while.

"I hear there are so many apple trees now, they cut them down in places—they call it 'thinning,' don't they?—and then plant things like potatoes instead.''

"Maybe it depends on where you are. I've never heard of them doing anything like that around here.''

Behind the river's embankment was an apple orchard; the powdery white flowers were in full bloom. Whenever I see apple blossoms I can smell the white face powder women use for makeup.

"Thanks for sending me all those apples, Keiko. . . . So I hear you're going to get married?''

"Yes,'' she nodded gravely, without a trace of bashfulness.

"When? Soon?''

"The day after tomorrow.''

"What!''

I was amazed. Keiko, however, acted quite unconcerned, as if the matter had nothing to do with her.

"Let's go back. You must have a million things to do.''

"No, not a thing.''

She was quite casual about it. I felt a secret admiration for her: she was an only child, her husband would be adopted into her father's family, and the continuation of the family line depended on her. Such people are clearly different, even if they are only nineteen or twenty years old.

"Tomorrow I'm going to Kodomari.'' As we recrossed the long bridge on our way back, I talked about other things. "I'm thinking of going to see Take.''

"Take? That would be the Take you wrote about in your story?''

"Yes.''

"That should make her glad, don't you think?''

"I don't know, but it would be nice if I could see her.''

Take was someone whom I particularly wanted to meet during this trip to Tsugaru. I think of her as my own mother. It was close to thirty years since I last saw her, but I had not forgotten her face. I might even say that it is because of her that my life has any direction at all. Here is another passage from "Memories":

I have clear memories too from the time when I was about six or seven. A maid called Take had taught me to read, and together we made our way through several books. Take gave herself over to the task of teaching me. As I was a sickly boy, I read many books in bed. When I ran out of books, Take would go and borrow more—from the Sunday school, for instance—and bring them to me. Because I had learned to read to myself, I never got tired, no matter how many books she brought.

Take also taught me about good and evil. She would often take me to the temple and explain the scrolls with the pictures of heaven and hell. Arsonists had baskets ablaze with red flames bound to their backs; adulterers were crushed by two-headed, green snakes coiled around their bodies; in pools of blood, on mountains of needles, in smoke-wreathed bottomless pits marked "Hell," everywhere wan and withered people were screaming through tiny cracks of mouths. When Take told me that I would go to hell if I lied, and that the demons would then pull out my tongue the way they did in the picture, I was so terrified I burst into tears.

The slight elevation behind the temple had been made into a graveyard, with a forest of grave markers standing alongside a hedge of yellow roses. Among the markers stood what looked like a black, iron cart wheel, about the size of a full moon. Take said that anyone turning the wheel would go to heaven if the wheel stopped dead, but if it stopped for just a moment and then rattled back in the opposite direction, he would go to hell. When she spun it, the wheel would turn smoothly for a good while and invariable stop dead, but when I tried it, it would sometimes turn back. I remember I went to the temple by myself, one autumn day, but no matter how many times I spun the wheel, it always rattled back on its tracks, as if it had been told to do so. I was getting tired and ready to throw a fit, but I stubbornly kept on turning, dozens of times. Then it grew dark, so I gave up in despair and left the graveyard. . . .

In due course I entered the village elementary school, and with that the nature of my recollections changes. Take disappeared without warning. She had found a husband in a fishing village and she must have been afraid I would try to follow her, for she left suddenly, without a word to me. It was the following year, during the Festival of the Dead, I believe, that she visited our house again, but for some reason she cold-shouldered me. She asked me about my grades. I did not answer. Someone else told her. Take had no special words of praise. All she did was warn me that you're never in greater danger than when you think you're safe.

Because my mother was in poor health, I never drank a drop of her milk, but was given to a wet nurse as soon as I was born. When I was two years old and tottering about on my own, I was taken away from her and put in the care of a nanny—Take. At night I would sleep in my aunt's arms, but during the day I was always with Take. For the next five years, until I was about seven, she raised me.

And then one morning I opened my eyes and called for Take, but Take did not come. I was shocked. Instinctively I knew what had happened. I wailed: "Take has gone! Take has gone!" I sobbed, feeling as if my heart would break; and for two or three days all I could do was cry. Even today I have not forgotten the pain of that moment. And then a year passed before I chanced to meet her again, but Take behaved in such a strange, standoffish way that I was left feeling wretched and bitter.

I hadn't seen her since. Four or five years ago I was asked to do a radio program called "A Few Words for My Hometown," and on that occasion I read those passages about Take from "Memories." When I hear the word "hometown," I remember Take. Presumably she was not listening to the radio at the time. I heard nothing from her.

Thus the matter had rested, but from the moment I set out on this trip I had a burning desire to see Take again, even if it were just for one moment. I take a secret pleasure in exercising self-control and postponing the best things until last. I had kept my visit to Kodomari, where Take lives, for the very end. In fact, I had considered going from Goshogawara to Hirosaki first, to walk around the streets and spend one night at a hot spring in Ōwani, thus postponing my visit to Kodomari yet a bit longer, but I had taken with me from Tokyo only a very small sum for traveling expenses, and that was starting to run low. I was also finally beginning to feel tired after all this traveling; the prospect of more walking had lost its charm. So I changed my plans, giving up on Ōwani altogether and deciding to stop off in Hirosaki on my way back to Tokyo. I would ask my aunt to put me up for the night and from Goshogawara go directly to Kodomari the following day.

When Keiko and I arrived at the house in Haikara-chō, my aunt was out. One of her grandchildren was in the hospital in Hirosaki, and she had gone there to keep the child company.

"Mother knew you were coming, so she telephoned: she very much wants to see you, and she asked you to stop by at the hospital in Hirosaki," her eldest daughter said with a smile. My aunt had married her off to a doctor who had been adopted into the family so as to continue the family line.

"Fine. I was planning to stop off in Hirosaki anyway on my way back to Tokyo, so I'll be sure to go and see her at the hospital."

"He says he's going to Kodomari tomorrow to see Take."

Although she must have been very busy with the preparations for her wedding, Keiko stayed with us as if she had nothing else to be doing.

"To see Take." My cousin looked serious. "That's good. She'll be so happy."

My cousin seemed to know how much I had been longing all these years to meet Take again.

"Though I wonder whether I'll be able to find her. . . ."

That worried me. I had, of course, made no arrangements at all. Koshino Take in Kodomari, this was all the information I had to go by.

"I heard there is only one bus a day for Kodomari."

Keiko had got up and was checking the timetable, which was pasted on the kitchen wall.

"If you don't get on the first train tomorrow, you won't be in time for the bus from Nakasato. Don't oversleep now, on such an important day."

She seemed to have forgotten completely about her own important day.

I would have to catch the first train from Goshogawara at 8:00 A.M., on the Tsugaru Railroad, north through Kanagi, as far as Nakasato where it ends. I would reach there at 9:00 A.M., and then get on the bus for Kodomari; the bus ride would take about two hours. In all probability I would arrive at Kodomari by about noon.

It was getting dark, and at long last Keiko went home. Just as she was leaving, Doctor (that was what we'd always called my cousin's husband, as if it were his name) came back from the hospital, and I drank with him and talked all sorts of nonsense till late that night.

The next day I was awakened by my cousin. I wolfed down my breakfast, ran to the station, and was just in time for the first

156

train. The weather was again clear, but my head was foggy; I felt hung over. There had been no one to fear at my aunt's, so I had drunk a little too much the night before. Drops of greasy sweat stood on my brow. With the clear morning sun shining into the train, the feeling that I alone exuded filth, impurity, and corruption was almost too much to bear. Thousands of times I have experienced this kind of self-loathing, which I always get after drinking too much. So far it has not resulted in a decision to put a resolute stop to my drinking, although others tend to look down on me because of my weakness for alcohol. Gazing blankly at the Tsugaru Plain through the train window, I seriously contemplated the ludicrous idea that, but for the existence of alcohol in this world, I might have been a saint. Before long we passed through Kanagi and arrived at Ashino Park, a station so small it looks like a flagman's shed.

Once, the mayor of Kanagi, who was returning from Tokyo, asked at Ueno Station for a ticket to Ashino Park. On being told that there was no such station, he demanded indignantly whether they had never heard of Ashino Park on the Tsugaru Railroad. He made the station employee check for at least half an hour until he finally got the ticket. I recalled that old anecdote as I stuck my head out of the window to look at the tiny station. A young girl dressed in a blue, splashed-pattern cotton kimono and baggy cotton pants came running to the ticket gate, clutching a big cloth-wrapped bundle in her arms and clenching her ticket between her teeth. Her eyes lightly closed, she offered her head to the handsome young ticket collector, who knew precisely what to do: deftly, with the movement of a skilled dentist extracting a tooth, he applied his puncher to the red ticket stuck between those rows of pearly teeth. Neither the girl nor the boy smiled for a moment. They behaved as if this were the most common thing in the world. No sooner had the girl climbed on than the train chugged off again, as though the engineer had been waiting for her. There can be few stations anywhere in the country quite as Arcadian. The mayor of Kanagi ought to shout "Ashino Park" more loudly next time he is in Ueno Station.

The train ran through a grove of larch trees. This area has become Kanagi's park. It has a pond, Rush Lake, for which my eldest brother once donated a pleasure boat, I believe.

Soon we arrived in Nakasato, a small community with a population of about four thousand. Because the Tsugaru Plain grows narrower from here on and villages further to the north such as Uchigata, Aiuchi, or Wakimoto have far fewer rice fields, I suppose one can call Nakasato the northern gate to the Tsugaru Plain. When I was very young I once stayed here with some relatives named Kanamaru, who owned a draper's shop, but I must have been about four at the time, and apart from the waterfall just outside the village I don't remember a thing.

"Shūji!"

Someone was calling my name, and when I looked around, there stood one of the Kanamaru girls, with a big smile on her face. She is one or two years older than I, but she doesn't look her age.

"It's been such a long time. What are you doing here?"

"I'm on my way to Kodomari." I was in a hurry to meet Take, and everything else left me cold. "This is my bus. Must be off, sorry."

"I see. Please stop by on your way back then. We've built a new house on top of that hill."

When I looked where she was pointing, I saw the house on top of a green hill to the right of the station. If it had not been for Take, I would have been glad at this chance meeting with a childhood playmate and would certainly have accepted her hospitality to listen in comfort to all the news about Nakasato. But I was in a ridiculous hurry. I felt as if I had not a moment to lose.

"Well, see you," I said casually, and quickly got on the bus.

The bus was crowded and I stood for the two hours or so it took to reach Kodomari.

This was the first time I had ever been to the countryside north of Nakasato. I have mentioned before that the Andō family, who are reputed to be the ancestors of the lords of Tsugaru, used to live around here, and that Jūsan used to be a bustling port, so the historical center of the Tsugaru Plain must have been here, between Nakasato and Kodomari. The bus continued north, climbing through the hills. The road was bad, and we rattled about a good deal. I held on firmly to the pole next to the luggage rack and peered with bent back through the windows at the scenery.

It was the north of Tsugaru all right—much wilder than, say, the landscape around Fukaura. Here, there was none of the smell of people. The shrubs and trees on the mountains, the brambles and bamboo grass, grow as if there were no intercourse between them and mankind. It is far more gentle than the landscape around Tappi on the east coast, but still, the plants and trees here have stopped just short of becoming "scenery." They have no words for the traveler.

Soon the shivery whiteness of Lake Jūsan unfolded before my eyes. It is like water served in a shallow oyster shell—graceful, but ephemeral. Not a boat, not a ripple disturbed its surface. It is still and large, a lonely expanse of water abandoned by human beings. It gives the impression that its surface would never reflect the shadows of scudding clouds or birds in flight.

Immediately beyond Lake Jūsan lies the Japan Sea shore, and because from here on we enter an area that is important to our national defense, I think it would be better again to avoid too detailed a description.

A little before noon I arrived in Kodomari, the last port on Honshu's west coast. Immediately to the north, across the mountains, lies Tappi on the east coast of Tsugaru. There are no villages beyond here on the west coast. If we take Goshogawara as the pivot, I had followed the movement of a pendulum clock and swung from Fukaura, the southernmost port of the old Tsugaru domain, straight to the northernmost port on the same coast, Kodomari.

Kodomari is a small fishing village with a population of about twenty-five hundred, but apparently already in the Kamakura period vessels from other provinces used to call here, and in particular boats bound for Hokkaido would invariably anchor here to shelter from the strong eastern winds. I believe I have mentioned several times already how in the Edo period Kodomari and the nearby port of Jūsan prospered as loading ports for rice and timber. Nowadays the harbor seems too grand for a mere village. There only are a very few rice fields, just outside the village, but there is an abundance of sea products: redfish, greenling, squid, and sardines, and also tangle, *wakame*, and many other kinds of seaweed.

"You wouldn't happen to know someone called Koshino Take, would you?" As soon as I got off the bus, I collared a passer-by and put my question to him.

"Koshino, Take, you said?" He was a middle-aged man dressed in the national civilian uniform who looked as if he might be a civil servant. He inclined his head as he thought. "There are lots of people called Koshino in this village."

"She used to live in Kanagi before she moved here. And she must be about fifty now." I was on tenterhooks.

"Ah, I know. If that's who you're looking for, she's here."

"She is? Where does she live? Where's her house?"

I walked in the direction I'd been shown and found Take's house. It was a neat little hardware store, with a shop front about five meters wide. It was at least ten times better than my own hovel in Tokyo. The shop curtain was drawn.

"Oh no!" I thought, and ran to the glass door at the entrance, but of course it was locked, with a small padlock. I tried to open the other glass doors, but they had all been locked securely. Take was out.

At a loss, I mopped the sweat off my brow. Take had moved! No, she couldn't have. Had she just slipped out for a moment? No, this was not Tokyo. Country people don't draw the shop curtains and lock up if they're just stepping out. Had she gone away for a few days, or perhaps even longer? It was no good; Take was away in some other village. Such things happen. I had been a fool to think that everything would be fine once I found her house. I tried tapping on the glass doors and calling.

"Mrs. Koshino! Mrs. Koshino!"

I never really expected an answer. With a deep sigh I walked away from the house and entered the tobacconist's across the street.

"There doesn't seem to be anyone in at Mrs. Koshino's. You wouldn't happen to know where she's gone?"

The emaciated old woman who ran the store casually answered that she guessed Mrs. Koshino had gone to the athletic meet. I felt a surge of hope.

"Where's this meet being held? Is it near, or . . . ?"

She said it was very near.

"Just go straight down this road until you come out into the rice fields and you'll see a school. The meet's being held behind it. She went this morning with her children, and she was carrying a lunch box."

"Really? Thank you very much."

I followed her directions and found the rice fields, and when I followed the path between the paddies I arrived at a sand dune, on top of which stood the elementary school. But when I walked around to the back, I was flabbergasted. This is what people must mean when they say they feel as if they are dreaming.

In this fishing village on Honshu's northern tip I saw—right there in front of me—a festival exactly like those of olden days, so beautiful and gay it almost brought tears to my eyes. Thousands of Japanese flags. Girls wearing their best clothes. Here and there drunken revelers, even though it was still broad daylight. And all around the field close to a hundred little booths—or rather, it looked as if there was not enough room around the field, and so even on the top of a low hill overlooking the tracks there were booths, with walls made of closely fitting straw mats. It was the noon break, and whole families had opened their lunch boxes in these hundred or so little houses. The men were drinking, the women and children were eating, and everyone was talking and laughing in the best of spirits.

I felt from the bottom of my heart that it was good to be Japanese; that this is really the Land of the Rising Sun. Even though we are involved in a war in which the fate of our whole nation is at stake, a remote village in the extreme north of Honshu had organized this delightful feast. I imagined that what I heard and saw before me was the good-humored laughter and dancing of the ancient gods. I felt like the hero of a fairy tale who has crossed seas and mountains and walked three thousand leagues in search of his mother, and who sees a beautiful sacred dance performed on top of a dune on the borders of the land to which he has been traveling.

Among this cheerful, dancing crowd I had to search for the mother who had brought me up. It was almost thirty years ago that we parted. She had big eyes and red cheeks. Over her right eyelid—or was it her left?—she had a tiny red mole. That was all I could remember. If I saw her, I would know her. Of that much I was sure, but as I looked around it almost made me cry to think how difficult it would be to find her in this crowd. Like a needle in a haystack.

I wandered aimlessly around the field.

"You wouldn't perhaps know where I might find Koshino Take?" I asked a boy, screwing up all my courage. "She's about fifty years old and has a hardware store.'' That was all I knew about my Take.

"Koshino, hardware store. . . .'' The boy thought for a moment. "Ah, I think she was in one of those booths over there.''

"Really? Over there, you said?''

"Well . . . I'm not quite certain. I just have a feeling I saw her somewhere. But anyway, have a look.''

Have a look—what a task that was going to be. Of course I couldn't unburden myself to the boy, how I hadn't seen her for thirty years, and so on. I would be making a spectacle of myself.

I thanked him and wandered off in the direction he had so vaguely indicated, but I did not expect to be any the wiser for it. Finally I stuck my head into a booth and disturbed a family in the middle of their lunch.

"Excuse me. Er . . . sorry to trouble you, but . . . Koshino Take. . . . I mean, Mrs. Koshino of the hardware store. . . . She wouldn't be here by any chance?''

"Not here,'' a fat woman, the owner of the booth, said with a sullen look.

"Is that so? I'm sorry to have troubled you. You haven't seen her perhaps, have you?''

"Well, I wouldn't know. There are a lot of people around here, you know.''

I looked into another booth and asked again.

They did not know.

And another booth.

As if possessed, I walked at least twice around the field, inquiring, "Is Take here? Take of the hardware store, is she here?'' No one could help me.

My hangover made me so thirsty I couldn't stand it any longer, and I went over to the school well to drink. Then I returned to the field, sat down on the sand, took off my jumper, wiped off the sweat, and stared vacantly at the crowd of young and old, men and women, all happiness and noise.

She is among them. She is certainly here—at this very moment, not knowing how I am suffering, perhaps opening her lunch box and feeding the children.

I wondered if I should go up to one of the teachers and ask him to page her with a megaphone—"Mrs. Koshino Take! A visitor to see you!"—but to resort to such drastic means did not appeal to me at all. It went against the grain to base my joy on an exaggerated stratagem that could be taken as a practical joke. Luck was simply not with me. The gods had decreed that we should not meet. Let's go back.

I put my jumper on and got up. Following the same path between the rice fields, I returned to the village. The meet would be over at about four o'clock. Another four hours, so why not find an inn where I could lie down for a while until Take came home? I thought about this, but if I had to wait those four hours all by myself in a filthy room in an inn, wouldn't I get fed up and lose my enthusiasm for meeting Take? I wanted to meet her feeling as I did now. But no matter what I tried, I was unable to find her. In short, I was out of luck.

To have come all this way to see her, to have found out immediately where she was, but to go home without having been able to meet her—perhaps it was an outcome befitting the bungled life I have been leading all these years. The plans I make so ecstatically invariably end up in a shambles, like now. I was born under an unlucky star. Let's go back!

When one thinks about it, she may have been my foster mother, but, to put it plainly, she was only a servant, a maid. Are you the child of a maid? A grown-up man yearning for his old nanny and wanting to meet her—just for one moment, please! No wonder you're a hopeless case! No wonder your brothers write you off as lowbred and spineless. Why among all your brothers and sisters are you alone such a disgusting spectacle? Pull yourself together, will you!

I went to the bus station and asked for the timetable. There was a bus leaving for Nakasato at 1:30 P.M., and it was the last one of the day. I decided to catch it. But as I still had about thirty minutes and had begun to feel hungry, I entered a dreary inn near the bus station and asked whether they could fix me a quick lunch. I was still undecided, and deep in my heart I was thinking that if this inn seemed nice I might just ask them to let me stay there until four o'clock. But I was sent packing.

"Everyone's gone to the meet. We're closed today," was the curt reply I got from the landlady, who appeared a bit sickly as she peeped out from behind the door.

More resolved than ever to go home, I sat down on the bench at the bus station and waited for ten minutes or so. Then I got up again and sauntered around a bit. I'll go past Take's empty house once more, I thought, and bid her an unseen farewell for this life. With a bitter smile I walked up to the hardware store, but then I noticed that the padlock had been removed. And the door had been pushed open a crack.

Heaven be praised! A sudden rush of courage overtook me and I pushed the glass door open with such vigor that it made a most inelegant rasping sound.

"Is there anybody home? Anybody home?"

"Yes," came the answer from inside, and a fourteen- or fifteen-year-old girl dressed in a sailor's suit stuck her head around the corner.

When I saw her face, it immediately brought to mind Take's. I had already lost all my shyness and walked over to where the girl stood, at the far end of the dirt-floor entrance.

"My name is Tsushima, from Kanagi," I introduced myself.

"Ah."

She smiled. Take must have told her children about the Tsushima child she had raised—how else could you explain the fact that already there was not a trace of the formality of strangers between the girl and me. I was grateful for it. I am Take's child. Even if that means I am the child of a maid or whatever, I don't care! I'll say it out loud: I am Take's child. I don't care if my brothers laugh at me. I am this girl's brother.

"Thank heavens!" I exclaimed impulsively. "And Take? Still at the meet?"

"Yes," she nodded calmly, not in the least on her guard or embarrassed by my presence. "I've got a tummy ache and so I came back just now to get some medicine."

I was sorry for her, but that tummy ache was most fortunate. I blessed that tummy ache. Now that I had found this girl, I was all right. I would meet Take for sure. No matter what, I would stick to this girl and not let her out of my sight.

"I walked all around the field looking for her, but I couldn't find her."

"I see," she nodded lightly, holding her stomach.

"Does it still hurt?"

"A little," she said.

"Did you take your medicine?"

She nodded.

"Does it hurt very much?"

She smiled and shook her head.

"In that case I would like to ask you a favor. Could you take me to Take? I know your tummy hurts, but I've come from far away. Can you walk?"

"Of course," she nodded vigorously.

"Good for you. Well, then, if you don't mind. . . ."

She nodded twice, and right away stepped down onto the dirt floor, slipped into her clogs, and left the house, her hands pressed on her stomach and her body bent forward a little.

"Did you run at the games?"

"Yes."

"Did you win a prize?"

"No."

Still clutching her stomach, she walked briskly ahead of me. Again we took the narrow path between the paddies, came out at the sand dune, walked around to the back of the school, cut straight across the sports field, and then the girl broke into a trot, entered a booth, and no sooner had she gone in than Take came out.

Take looked at me, her eyes expressionless.

"I'm Shūji," I smiled, and took off my cap.

"Never!"

That was all she said. She did not even smile. She looked grave. But soon she shed her stiffness, and said in a weak voice that sounded casual and strangely resigned:

"Well, shall we go inside and watch the games?"

She led me into her booth.

"Won't you sit down here, please?"

I found myself sitting next to Take, and from that moment on she did not speak a word, but sat perfectly straight, both hands properly placed on the round knees of her baggy pants, and looked intently at the children's races. Still, I was completely happy. I felt utterly secure. My legs stretched out in front of me, I watched the games, my mind completely vacant. I felt absolutely devoid of cares and worries, and without the slightest concern for what might happen next.

Is this the kind of feeling that is meant by "peace"? If it is, I can say that my heart experienced peace then for the first time in my life. My real mother, who died a few years ago, was an extremely noble, gentle, and good mother, yet she never gave me this strange feeling of reassurance. I wonder: do the mothers of this world all give their children this rest, the rest of a mind that can be at peace because Mother will always be there to help? If this is so, then the desire at all costs to be good to one's parents springs naturally from this feeling. I cannot understand how some people can fall sick or idle their time away while they have this wonderful thing, a mother. Filial piety is a natural emotion, not an imposed code of conduct.

I was right: Take's cheeks are red, and over her right eyelid is a little red mole about the size of a poppy seed. Her hair is streaked with silver, but the way she sits up straight, here by my side, Take is not a bit different from the Take I remember from my childhood. She told me this, later, but when she went into service with my family and carried me around, I was two and she was thirteen. She looked after my upbringing and education for no longer than the next six years, and yet the Take I remember is no young girl at all, but a mature person in no way different from the Take I now see before me. And this, too, is something she told me afterward, but the dark blue sash with the iris pattern she is wearing now is the same one she used to wear when she was in our service, and the light purple neckpiece under her kimono, this too she received from my parents, at about the same time. Isn't this why Take, as she sits here, seems exactly as I remember her?

Perhaps I am biased, but it seems to me that Take is a cut above the other *aba* (feminine of *aya*) of this village. She is wearing a new kimono of handwoven striped cotton and baggy trousers of the same material, and this striped pattern is of course far from stylish, but still, it has been chosen with taste. It doesn't look funny. In every respect she gives a—what shall I say?—an impression of strength.

I sat there, never speaking a word. Some time passed. Then Take, staring straight ahead of her at the races, heaved a long, deep sigh that shook her shoulders. That was when I first understood that Take too was less than composed. Yet she was silent.

And then, as if it had suddenly occurred to her, she asked me:

"Won't you have something to eat?"

"No, thanks," I answered. I really didn't want a thing.

"I've got some rice cakes."

Take reached out for the lunch box, which she had tucked away in a corner of the booth.

"Please don't bother. I don't want to eat."

She nodded lightly and did not press me further.

"I see. It's not rice cakes you want," she said softly, smiling.

We hadn't been in touch for close to thirty years, but it seemed as if she could tell I like my drink. It was uncanny. I grinned, but Take frowned.

"And you smoke too! You haven't stopped smoking since you got here. I taught you to read, but never to smoke or drink, did I?"

You're never in greater danger than when you think you're safe—oh yes! I stopped grinning.

Now that I was looking serious, it was Take's turn to smile. She got up.

"Shall we go and look at the Dragon God's cherry blossoms? How would that be?" she said invitingly.

"Oh yes, let's."

I followed Take up the sand dune behind the booth. The violets on the dune were in full bloom. Low-hanging wisteria vines were creeping in all directions. Take climbed in silence. Without a word, I plodded on behind her. We reached the top, and then trudged down the other side until we arrived at the Grove of the Dragon God. Here and there double cherry blossoms bloomed along the little lane. Take suddenly reached out and broke off a blossom-laden branch. As she walked along, she plucked off blossom after blossom and threw them to the ground. Then she stopped in her tracks, turned around forcefully, and burst into a flood of words, as if a dam had broken.

"What a long time it's been! At first I didn't understand. 'Tsushima from Kanagi,' my daughter said, but I thought she must be mistaken. Of course I never imagined you'd come to visit me. And when I came out of the booth and saw your face, I still didn't recognize you. 'I'm Shūji,' you said, and I thought, Never!, and then my tongue tied itself in a knot. I couldn't see the races any more, or anything else. For almost thirty years I've been wanting to meet you again, and all those years I was thinking, Shall I be able to see him again or not? And then to think you've grown up to be such a fine, big man and come all the way to Kodomari because you wanted to see Take, it makes me grateful and glad and sad, I don't know which, but I'm so happy you're here! When I went into service with your family, you could hardly walk: you'd totter a few steps and tumble, totter, totter, and tumble. And when it was time to eat you'd walk around with a rice bowl in your hands, and you liked best of all to eat your meals at the bottom of the stone steps of the storehouse, making me tell you stories and feed you spoon by spoon while you stared at me with your big, round eyes. You were a lot of trouble, but you were so sweet, and here you are such a big man . . . it all seems like a dream. I went back sometimes to Kanagi, and walked down the streets wondering whether you might not be playing somewhere. I'd look at every single boy that seemed about your age. Oh, I'm so glad you're here!"

At every word she spoke, she plucked and dropped, plucked and dropped, the blossoms from the branch in her hand, as if in a trance.

"Do you have any children?" At long last she snapped the branch and dropped it too. She stuck out her elbows and gathered up her trousers and adjusted them. "How many children?"

I leaned against a cedar beside the lane and answered that I had one.

"A boy or a girl?"

"A girl."

"How old?"

And she fired off question after question.

When I saw how strongly and freely she showed her affection, I realized how like her I am. It dawned on me that it is as a result of her influence, of the influence of this dear foster mother, that I alone of all my brothers and sisters have such a rustic, such an uncouth side to my character. For the first time I was confronted with the way in which I had been raised. I am certainly not the product of a refined upbringing. No wonder I wasn't a typical rich kid. For consider: the people I shall never be able to forget are my friend T. in Aomori, Mr. Nakabata in Goshogawara, Aya in Kanagi, and Take in Kodomari. Aya still works for the family, but all the others also served with us at one time or another. I am their friend.

Far be it from me to pretend to emulate the old sage's last, dying poem about the griffin hunt, but here is not such a bad point for your author to lay down his pen and end this wartime *New Tsugaru Gazetteer* with the profession that he caught, not griffins, but friends.[2]

Many things remain that I would like to write about, but I feel that in these pages I have more or less said all I could about the spirit of Tsugaru. I did not exaggerate. I did not deceive my readers.

Well then, reader, let us meet again, if we live. Let us keep our spirits up. Do not despair. Goodbye.

1 (p. 137)   The characters *ki-zukuri* (木造) are usually read *moku-zō*, which means "made of wood."

2 (p. 171)   *The old sage*. There is a legend that Confucius died while he was writing a poem about hunting griffins in the west.

APPENDIX I
Works cited by Dazai

"An Account of Jūsan" ("*Jūsan ōrai*"). Dazai's collective name for a series of historical accounts and descriptions of the Tsugaru region, written by various hands during the Edo period and used as an educational textbook. Actually only one of these accounts was called "*Jūsan ōrai*," and it did not furnish the quotation on p. 125, which was taken from a section called "*Koseki*," "Historic Sites."

Asagao Diary (*Asagao nikki*, or *Shō utsushi asagaobanashi*), 1832. Posthumous puppet play by Chikamatsu Tokusō (1751–1810).

Chronicle of the Nine Generations of Hōjō Regents (*Hōjō kudaiki*). Anonymous chronicle of unknown date covering the years 1183–1332.

Companion to History (*Dokushi biyō*). Published in 1933 by the Tokyo University Institute for the Compilation of Historiographical Materials.

"The Dandy's Progress" ("*Oshare dōji*"), 1939. A short story by Dazai. Translated by James Westerhoven, *Bulletin of the Faculty of Education of Hirosaki University*, No. 48 (Sept. 1982), 2–7.

Ei-kei War Chronicle (*Ōu Ei-Kei gunki*, or *Chronicle of the War in Ōu from the Eiroku to the Keichō Era*, i.e. from 1558–69 to 1596–1614). Published in 1698 by Tobe Masanao (1645–1707). In Eiroku 5 (1562), the emperor commissioned Oda Nobunaga to restore order around the capital, thus starting a train of events that culminated in the Battle of Sekigahara in Keichō 5 (1600).

"Going Home" ("*Kikyōrai*"), 1943. A short story by Dazai.

History of Aomori Prefecture (*Aomori-ken tsūshi*), 1941. By the Hirosaki historian Takeuchi Unpei (1881–1945).

Illustrated Encyclopedia of Japan and China (*Wakan sansai zue*), 1712. Based on a Chinese encyclopedia (*San-tsai tu-hui*) of 1610.

Introduction to the Industries of Ōshū (*Ōshū sangyō sōsetsu*), by Satō Hiroshi (1897–1962), professor of geography at Hitotsubashi University. Possibly the title of a chapter in a reference work.

Kasoku Chronicle (*Kasoku-ki*), by Kasoku, a younger brother of Nobumasa, fourth lord of Hirosaki.

Kidate Diary (*Kidate nikki*, also called *Tsugaru rekiseiroku*), edited in 1775 by Kidate Yōzaemon Morisada.

Konjaku monogatari. A collection of didactic tales ascribed to Minamoto no Takakuni (1004–77), with later additions by other hands. Marian Ury has translated sixty-nine of its stories (*Tales of Things Now Past*, University of California Press, 1979), but not the one referred to on p. 105.

The Love Suicides at Amijima (*Shinjū ten no Amijima*), 1721. One of the most famous plays by the greatest writer for the puppet drama, Chikamatsu Monzaemon (1653–1725). Translated by Donald Keene in *Four Major Plays by Chikamatsu* (Columbia University Press, 1961).

Man'yōshū, late eighth century. The oldest extant compilation of Japanese poetry. It has never been translated in its entirety, but selections may be found in many anthologies, notably Robert H. Brower and Earl Miner's *Japanese Court Poetry* (Stanford University Press, 1961).

Masukagami (*Greater Mirror* or *Clear Mirror*), an anonymous late fourteenth-century chronicle covering the years 1183–1333. The poem that N. suddenly switches to (p. 93) concludes the introduction to the work: "Writing now my own account of past events, / I will record the deeds of ancient days / In this clear mirror, this *Masukagami*."

The M-Company Brawl (*Me-gumi no kenka*), 1890. Kabuki play by Takeshiba Kisui (1847–1923) concerning a quarrel between a company of firemen and a group of sumo wrestlers.

"Memories" ("*Omoide*"), 1933. Dazai's first major publication. Translated by James O'Brien in *Dazai Osamu: Selected Stories and Sketches* (Cornell University Press, 1983).

"My Hometown" ("*Kokyō*"), 1943. A newspaper feature by Dazai.

Narrow Road to a Far Land (*Oku no hosomichi*), 1694. The last and most famous haiku travelogue by Matsuo Bashō (1644–94). Translated by Dorothy Britton as *A Haiku Journey* (Tokyo: Kodansha International, 1975).

Nozaki Village (*Nozaki mura*). A famous scene from the puppet play *Shinpan Utazaimon* (1780) by Chikamatsu Hanji (1725–83).

Precepts for Pilgrims (*Angya okite*). Attributed to Bashō, but almost certainly apocryphal. First recorded in 1760.

Records of a Journey to the East (*Tōyūki*), 1795, sequel published 1798. Companion volume to *Record of a Journey to the West* (*Saiyūki*), 1795, sequel 1797, by Tachibana Nankei (1753–1805), who traveled around Japan between 1782 and 1788.

"Sanshō the Steward" ("*Sanshō dayū*"), 1915. One of the most famous stories by Mori Ōgai (1862–1922). It has been translated into many languages and in 1954 was made into a film by Mizoguchi Kenji, under the title *Sanshō the Bailiff*. Translated by J. Thomas Rimer in *The Incident at Sakai and Other Stories*, eds. David Dilworth and J. Thomas Rimer (University Press of Hawaii, 1977).

Shoku-Nihongi (*Continuation of the Chronicles of Japan*), 795. Covers the years 697–792. Its principal editor was Sugeno Mamichi, d. 814.

Takaya Family Chronicle (*Takaya-ki* or *Tsugaru-ki*), 1664. Edited by Takaya Buzen Kiyonaga.

Tsubosaka reigenki, 1879. Puppet play by Toyozawa Danpei (1827–98).

APPENDIX II
List of personal and historical references

Abe no Hirafu. Governor of Koshi. Led an expedition against the Ezo in 658 and against Korea in 662.

Abe no Sadatō, 1019–62. Son of Abe no Yoritoki. His death meant the end of the Earlier Nine Years' War.

Abe no Yoritoki, d. 1057. Ruler of a vast territory in Mutsu. His unwillingness to obey the commands of the central government was one of the causes of the Earlier Nine Years' War, in one of whose battles he was killed.

Abe Sanesue, d. 1659. Lord of Akita until 1602, when he was transferred to a much smaller fief. Banished in 1632, he died in exile.

Akutagawa Ryūnosuke, 1892–1933. The well-known author of *Kappa*, ''Rashōmon,'' and other fiction. He was Dazai's literary idol, and his suicide made a deep impression on the younger writer.

Asaka Yasuhiko, 1887–1981. Member of a cadet branch of the imperial family. He married a daughter of Emperor Meiji, but lost his title of Imperial Prince after the Second World War.

Ba Maw, 1893–1977. First Prime Minister of British-administered Burma, later imprisoned by the British on sedition charges. Set up as Head of State by the Japanese Army in 1943.

Benkei. Also called Musashi-bō Benkei. Fighting monk of legendary strength and cunning. He is said to have been Minamoto no Yoshitsune's closest friend and armor bearer, and to have died with his lord. It is doubtful whether he is an actual historical personage.

Bokusui. Wakayama Bokusui, 1885–1928. Lyrical poet, whose favorite pastime was to ramble through nature with a bottle of *sake* in his rucksack. His example may have inspired Dazai. The complete text of the song N. sings on p. 93 is: "How many mountains and rivers / Must I cross to the land / Where loneliness ends? / Today again I travel on."

Bonchō, d. 1714. A disciple of Bashō and one of the editors of the *Saru mino* (*Monkey's Raincoat*, 1691), from which the haiku on p. 147 is taken: "In the city / What a heavy smell of things! / The summer moon." (Trans. Donald Keene, *World Within Walls.* Tokyo: Tuttle, 1976, p. 111).

Chichibu, 1902–53. Imperial Prince. Younger brother of Emperor Hirohito. Served with the Eighth Army Division in Hirosaki from August 1935 to December 1936.

Danrin School. School of poetry originally characterized by freedom and humor, later vulgarized. Its period of greatest bloom was 1675–85. Bashō was associated with it at the beginning of his career only.

Earlier Nine Years' War, 1051–62. Conflict in Mutsu, during which the Abe clan, who ruled most of that province, were defeated by Minamoto no Yoriyoshi and his son Yoshi'ie.

Ebisu or *Ezo.* Collective name for the uncivilized tribes that were not subjected to central rule until late. There were Ainu among them, but also ethnic Japanese.

Fujiwara no Hidehira, 1096–1187. Son of Motohira and third Fujiwara ruler of Hiraizumi. Supported the Minamoto side against the Taira and offered sanctuary to Yoshitsune when the latter was fleeing from his brother Yoritomo.

Fujiwara no Hidesato, fl. 939. Governor of Shimotsuke (now Tochigi Prefecture) and later military prefect of the north. Ancestor of the Fujiwara of Hiraizumi.

Fujiwara no Motohira, d. 1157. Son of Kiyohira, the founder of the Hiraizumi line.

Fujiwara no Yasuhira, d. 1189. Son of Hidehira. Trying to curry favor with Minamoto no Yoritomo, he attacked and killed Yoshitune at Takadate. Yoritomo in turn attacked and killed Yasuhira and divided his possessions among his Minamoto warriors.

Fujiwara no Yasunori, 825–895. General. Sent out against the Ezo in 878.

Fumiya no Watamaro, 763–821. Sakanoue no Tamuramaro's successor as shogun. Led an expedition against the Ezo in 812.

Genroku era, 1688–1704. A period of great cultural achievements, the Golden Age of the Tokugawa shogunate.

Go-Daigo, 1288–1339. Emperor from 1318, he tried to overthrow the Hōjō Regency in the Genkō uprising of 1331. He was deposed and exiled, but returned in 1333 and briefly succeeded in reestablishing direct imperial rule. In 1336 his authority was challenged by Ashikaga Taka'uji, and he withdrew to Mount Yoshino, south of Kyoto, where he established the Southern Dynasty. Because of his championship of imperial authority, Go-Daigo was a favorite of the post-Meiji nationalists.

Goncharov, Ivan Aleksandrovich, 1812–91. This well-known novelist served as secretary to the Russian mission to Japan of 1852–55. His recollections of his journey are recorded in *Fregat Pallada* (*The Frigate "Pallas,"* 1858), which may well have been the source of the passage referred to on p. 89–90.

Hōjō Takatoki, 1303–33. From 1311, regent of the Kamakura shogunate. Deserted by his partisans at the return of Emperor Go-Daigo in 1333, he committed ritual suicide.

Hyakusui. Hirafuku Hyakusui, 1877–1933. Painter from Akita.

Ichinohe Hyōei, 1855–1931. Born in Hirosaki. He distinguished himself in the wars with China and Russia. After his retirement from active service, he was president of the Peers' School (1920–22), and in 1924 was made chief priest of the Meiji Shrine.

Iki no Muraji Hakatoko. One of the compilers of the Taihō Code, a collection of laws promulgated in 701.

Izumi Kyōka, 1873–1939. Author of socialist, later romantic, novels.

Kamakura period, 1185–1333. Period between Minamoto no Yoritomo's defeat of the Taira family and Hōjō Takatoki's suicide.

Kamura Isota, 1897–1933. Novelist.

Kannon. Buddhist goddess of mercy.

Kasai Zenzō, 1887–1928. Naturalist novelist. Born in Hirosaki.

Kida Teikichi, 1871–1939. Eminent historian; professor of history at Kyoto Imperial University.

Kitabatake Akimura, 1557–78. Last lord of Namioka. Killed after a siege by the forces of Tsugaru Tamenobu.

Kōnin, 708–781. Emperor of Japan from 770.

Konoe Hisamichi, d. 1541. Court noble.

Konoe Sakihisa, 1536–1612. One of the most influential aristocrats of the age; appointed chancellor in 1582. Patron of Tsugaru Tamenobu.

Kunohe Masazane, d. 1591. Refused to submit to Toyotomi Hideyoshi and was besieged in Kunohe Castle near Fukuoka in Iwate Prefecture. He was beheaded after its fall.

Later Three Years' War, 1083–87. Conflict in Dewa, in which Minamoto no Yoshi'ie defeated Kiyohara no Iehira, the ruler of that province.

Masaoka Shiki, 1867–1902. Poet.

Minamoto no Yoritomo, 1147–99. First shogun of the Minamoto family. Assisted by his brother Yoshitsune, he decisively defeated the forces of the rival Taira family and by 1185 was undisputed ruler of most of Japan. Perhaps jealous of his brother's growing fame and popularity, Yoritomo declared Yoshitsune a traitor and ordered him arrested. Yoshitsune fled to Hiraizumi, where he was treacherously killed by Fujiwara no Yasuhira in 1189. Yoritomo then attacked Hiraizumi and soon extended his rule over the whole of the northeast. He was made shogun in 1192.

Minamoto no Yoshitsune, 1159–89. One of the most popular heroes in Japanese history. In 1180 he joined his brother Yoritomo's forces and with his brilliant tactics secured his family's victory over the Taira. Declared a traitor by his brother, he escaped to Hiraizumi, where he was offered sanctuary, but later was treacherously attacked. Yoshitsune committed suicide to escape capture, but a persistent legend claimed that he made his way to the continent via Hokkaido and continued his heroic career under the name Genghis Khan.

Muromachi period, 1392–1568. Period between the settlement of the conflict between the northern and southern dynasties and the fall of the Ashikaga shogunate.

Nagasune-hiko. Legendary native ruler of the Yamato region around Nara, which he tried to defend against the invading forces of the first emperor, Jinmu. This resistance cost him his life.

Nagatsuka Takashi, 1879–1915. Poet and novelist.

Naka no Ōe. Son of Empress Saimei, reigned himself as Emperor Tenji from 668–671.

Nanbu Family. Branch of the Takeda family which settled at Nanbu in Kōshū and took their name from that place. In 1189, Nanbu (or Takeda) Mitsuyuki received the domain of Sannohe in Aomori Prefecture from Minamoto no Yoritomo. His descendants resided there until 1598, when they transferred their seat to their new stronghold at Morioka in Iwate Prefecture. A cadet branch settled in Hachinohe, on the east coast of Aomori Prefecture. The rivalry between the Nanbu and Tsugaru clans is legendary.

Nanbu Takanobu, d. 1581. Brother of Nanbu Yasanobu, twenty-third lord of Sannohe. Lord of Ishikawa Castle, south of Hirosaki, from where he ruled Tsugaru. His power was gradually eroded by the growing power of Ōura (later Tsugaru) Tamenobu. Tsugaru historians claim that he committed suicide when his castle fell to the Ōura forces in 1571, but Nanbu partisans maintain he died of illness ten years later.

Ogawa Takuji, 1870–1941. Professor of geography at Kyoto Imperial University.

Ōura Mitsunobu, 1460–1526. Powerful local Tsugaru chieftain. Considered an ancestor of Tsugaru Tamenobu.

Ozaki Kōyō, 1867–1903. Novelist.

Po Chü-i, 772–846. One of the greatest poets of the Tang period and very popular in Japan.

Saigō Takamori, 1827–77. Proverbially honest and uncompromisingly idealistic leader. Played an important part in the Meiji Restoration, but withdrew from public life out of dissatisfaction with the policies of the new government; finally agreed to lead a group of discontented samurai in the Satsuma Rebellion. After his defeat, he committed suicide on the battlefield, near Kagoshima.

Saitō Ryoku'u, 1867–1904. Poet and novelist.

Sakanoue no Tamuramaro, 758–811. First shogun in the history of Japan (797). Led an expedition against the Ezo of the north in 794, and another one in 801.

Shukushin. Northern Chinese, perhaps Tungusic, tribes who raided the Japan Sea coasts in the sixth and seventh centuries.

Shōmu, 699–756. Emperor of Japan from 724 to 749.

Suian. Hirafuku Suian, 1844–90. Painter from Akita.

Taika Reform. A major reorganization of administration and landownership under Emperor Kōtoku, promulgated in 645.

Takuboku. Ishikawa Takuboku, 1886–1912. Renovator of the *tanka.* The whole song which N. renders so unfortunately on p. 93 goes: "On the silver shore / Of an islet in the eastern sea / My face streaked with tears / I frolic with the crabs."

Tokugawa Ieyasu, 1542–1616. The founder of the Tokugawa shogunate. He consolidated his power by winning the Battle of Sekigahara in 1600 and was appointed shogun in 1603. He abdicated two years later, but continued to rule in fact if not in name.

Tomo'emon. Ōtani Tomo'emon VI, 1886–1943. Famous kabuki actor. Succeeded to his stage name in 1920. Ume no Yoshibei, one of his great roles, is the main character of a play by Namiki Gohei (1747–1808).

Toyotomi Hideyori, 1593–1615. Son of Hideyoshi. Too young to rule personally at the death of his father, he became the symbol of the anti-Tokugawa party and a source of continuous concern for the newly established Tokugawa shogunate. In the summer of 1615, Tokugawa forces took Hideyori's residence at Osaka Castle after a siege. Hideyori committed suicide to avoid capture. His death removed the last threat to the Tokugawa family.

Toyotomi Hideyoshi, 1536–98. One of Oda Nobunaga's most brilliant generals. On Nobunaga's assassination in 1582, Hideyoshi moved quickly to assume Nobunaga's place as the most powerful lord in Japan. In this capacity he laid the ground rules for the centralization of the nation that was to be carried out by his Tokugawa successors. He had visions of subjecting Korea and China, but his invasions of Korea in 1592 and 1597 were unsuccessful.

Tsugaru Nobufusa, 1620–62. Second son of Nobuhira. Became first lord of Kuroishi in 1656.

Tsugaru Nobuharu, 1762–91. Succeeded his father Nobuyasu as eighth lord of Hirosaki in 1784.

Tsugaru Nobuhira, 1586–1631. Third son of Tamenobu. Succeeded his father as second lord of Hirosaki in 1607.

Tsugaru Nobumasa, 1646–1710. Invested as fourth lord of Hirosaki in 1658, three years after the death of his father Nobuyoshi. One of the "seven wise lords" of the Genroku era, the others being: Tokugawa Tsunaeda, lord of Mito; Maeda Tsunanori, lord of Kaga; Matsudaira Sadashige, lord of Kuwana and later of Takada in Echigo; Kuroda Tsunamasa, lord of Fukuoka; Hosokawa Tsunatoshi, lord of Kumamoto; and Mizuno Tadayuki, lord of Okazaki.

Tsugaru Nobuyasu, 1739–84. Succeeded his father Nobuaki as seventh lord of Hirosaki in 1744.

Tsugaru Tamenobu, 1550–1607. Founder of the Tsugaru clan. Probably descended from a minor branch of the Nanbu family. Revolted against Nanbu control over Tsugaru in 1571 and by 1588 had become the effective ruler of the whole region.

Tsugaru Tsuguakira, 1840–1916. Fourth son of the lord of Kumamoto. Became the twelfth and last lord of Hirosaki in 1857, when he married Yukitsugu's daughter. On the abolition of the feudal domains in 1871 he received the title of count.

Tsugaru Yasuchika, 1765–1833. Sixth lord of Kuroishi. Adopted by Nobuharu, whom he succeeded as ninth lord of Hirosaki in 1791. Retired in 1825.

Tsugaru Yukitsugu, 1800–65. Third son of the lord of Yoshida in Mikawa. Became ninth lord of Kuroishi through adoption in 1825, and in 1839 was made eleventh lord of Hirosaki on the forced retirement of his second adoptive father, Nobuyuki.

Wen-ti. Chinese emperor from 179 to 157 B.C.

Wu-ti. Chinese emperor from 140 to 87 B.C.

Yamato Takeru. Perhaps the most famous of Japan's legendary heroes. At the age of twenty-six, he was sent out by his father the emperor to put down a rebellion of the Ezo in the east; after a successful campaign he died on the way back. His death is traditionally dated in 113.

Yoshino period, 1336–92. Period between Emperor Go-Daigo's retreat from the capital and the settlement of the conflict between the northern and southern dynasties.

APPENDIX III
List of geographical names

Akita. Capital of Akita Prefecture and site of an ancient castle built in 733 to control the Ezo.

Asakusa. One of Tokyo's liveliest amusement centers.

Atami. Famous hot spring on the Izu Peninsula.

Bizen. Name of an ancient province on the Inland Sea; now part of Okayama Prefecture.

Dewa. Old province, corresponding more or less to the Japan Sea coast of northern Honshu, minus Tsugaru.

Eastern Sea Road (Tōkaidō). Trunk road that led from the capital (Nara, later Kyoto) east along the coast of the Pacific to Nakoso.

Eastern Mountain Road (Tōsandō). Followed a course parallel to the Eastern Sea Road, but more inland, skirting the mountains and ending at Shirakawa. Later both roads gave their names to provinces, or—more properly—circuits.

Echigo. Old province; now part of Niigata Prefecture, on the Japan Sea.

Echizen. Old province; now part of Fukui Prefecture, on the Japan Sea.

Ezo. Name for Hokkaido during the Edo period.

Hakata. Town in Kyushu, noted for its fine silk sashes.

Hiraizumi. Town in southern Iwate Prefecture, near the Pacific. From 1094 to 1189 it was the capital of a semi-independent principality under a branch of the Fujiwara.

Horikoshi. Now a southern suburb of Hirosaki. Site of an old stronghold of Tsugaru Tamenobu.

Iwaki. Highest mountain in Aomori Prefecture (alt. 1,625 meters, or 5,400 feet).

Iwaki. Old province on the Pacific coast, on the border of Fukushima and Miyagi prefectures.

Iwakidaira. Now Taira; town in Fukushima Prefecture.

Iwashiro. Old province, located east of Iwaki Province.

Izawa. Near Mizusawa in Iwate Prefecture. Site of a castle built by Sakanoue no Tamuramaro in 802, and seat of the military prefecture whose task it was to control the Ezo.

Kaga. Old province on the Japan Sea coast; now part of Ishikawa Prefecture.

Kamikita Mountains. Mountain range on the Pacific coast in Iwate Prefecture.

Kegon Falls. Spectacular waterfall near Nikkō, north of Tokyo.

Kikai Archipelago. Old name for the Ōsumi Islands, south of Kyushu.

Kishū. Better known as Kii. Old province, covering the coastal parts of the Kii Peninsula, south of Osaka.

Kiso. Mountainous region northeast of Nagoya.

Koishikawa. A comparatively quiet Tokyo neighborhood, known for its botanical garden.

Koshi. Ancient province, later divided into Echizen and Echigo.

Kōshū. Also known as Kai. Old province, now part of Yamanashi Prefecture, west of Tokyo. This region has long been famous for its vineyards and nowadays produces more than half the wine grown in Japan.

Kuji. Small town on the Pacific coast of Iwate Prefecture, said by some to have been the ancestral home of Tsugaru Tamenobu.

Kuwana. City on the Ise Bay, west of Osaka.

Matsumae. Town on the Tsugaru Strait in the southwest of Hokkaido. During the Edo period the most important port of Hokkaido and the seat of its ruling family, who built their castle there in 1601. The tidal wave mentioned on p. 72 occurred in 1741.

Nagoya in Hizen. Port in Saga Prefecture, Kyushu, from where Toyotomi Hideyoshi in 1592 launched his fleet against Korea. Not to be confused with the metropolis of the same name.

Nakoso. Town on the Pacific coast in Fukushima Prefecture.

Namioka. Small town between Hirosaki and Aomori City.

Naoe. Now Naoetsu, town on the Japan Sea coast in Niigata Prefecture.

Noshiro. Town on the Japan Sea coast, north of Akita city.

Ōdate in Kōzuke. Town in Gunma Prefecture, northwest of Tokyo.

Odawara. Castle town on the Pacific coast in Kanagawa Prefecture. Stronghold of the powerful Hōjō clan, who refused to recognize the overlordship of Toyotomi Hideyoshi.

Ōgaki. Town in Gifu Prefecture, just east of Sekigahara.

Ōmi. Old province; now part of Shiga Prefecture, east of Kyoto.

Ōshū. Other name for Mutsu Province, but sometimes used to indicate the whole of the northeast, which consists of Fukushima, Miyagi, Yamagata, Iwate, Akita, and Aomori prefectures.

Ōura. Site of an old castle of Tsugaru Tamenobu, west of Hirosaki.

Parhae. Also Pōhai. Ancient Korean kingdom and successor state to Koguryö. It existed from 713 to 926, and was situated on the east coast of North Korea, directly across the Japan Sea from Akita.

Satsuma, Chōshū, and Tosa. Three domains in the southwest of Japan. Samurai from these domains played an important part in the Meiji Restoration.

Screen Forest. Forest covering the Screen Hills, or Byōbu-zan, a dune formation along the Tsugaru west coast; so called not only because of its protective function, but also because of its shape, which resembles that of a folding chamber screen.

Sekigahara. Town in Gifu Prefecture, east of Kyoto. Site of a famous battle in 1600, in which Tokugawa Ieyasu gained the upper hand over his opponents and became in effect ruler of Japan.

Shinano. Old province, now part of Nagano Prefecture in central Honshu.

Shirakawa. Town in Fukushima Prefecture.

Shōnai Plain. Around the town of Tsuruoka, on the Japan Sea coast of Yamagata Prefecture.

Sumida River. Tokyo's most important river.

Taga. Near Sendai in Miyagi Prefecture. Site of an ancient castle built in 724 to control the Ezo.

Takadate. Also Takadachi. Yoshitsune's residence near Hiraizumi, where in 1189 he committed suicide to avoid capture.

Tappi. Name of the hamlet and cape at the northernmost tip of the Tsugaru Peninsula.

Tappi Pond. Large pond between Kanagi and the Japan Sea, not to be confused with the preceding, which is written with different characters.

Ugo. Old province, more or less identical with Akita Prefecture.

Utetsu. Hamlet just south of Tappi.

Wakasa. Old province on the Japan Sea, now part of Fukui Prefecture.

Yaku. One of the largest of the Ōsumi Islands south of Kyushu.

Yatate Pass. Border between Aomori and Akita prefectures, just south of Ikarigaseki.

Yugawara. Famous hot spring on the Izu Peninsula.

SUGGESTIONS FOR FURTHER READING

Dazai Osamu. *The Setting Sun*. Translated by Donald Keene. New York: New Directions, 1956; Tokyo: Tuttle, 1981.

————. *No Longer Human*. Translated by Donald Keene. New York: New Directions, 1958; Tokyo: Tuttle, 1981.

————. *Dazai Osamu: Selected Stories and Sketches*. Translated by James A. O'Brien. Ithaca, N.Y.: Cornell University Press, 1983 (East Asia Papers No. 33).

————. "Villon's Wife." Translated by Donald Keene. In *Modern Japanese Literature*, ed. Donald Keene. New York: Grove Press, 1956; Tokyo: Tuttle, 1957.

————. "The Courtesy Call." Translated by Ivan Morris. In *Modern Japanese Stories*, ed. Ivan Morris (Tokyo: Tuttle, 1962), and *The World of Japanese Fiction*, ed. Arthur O. Lewis and Yoshinobu Hakutani (New York: Dutton, 1973).

Donald Keene. "Dazai Osamu." In his *Landscapes and Portraits* (Tokyo: Kodansha International, 1971), reissued in paperback as *Appreciations of Japanese Culture* (Tokyo: Kodansha International, 1981).

Phyllis I. Lyons. *The Saga of Dazai Osamu: A Critical Study with Translations*. Stanford: Stanford University Press, 1985.

James A. O'Brien. *Dazai Osamu*. Boston: Twayne, 1975 (Twayne's World Authors Series No. 348).

Sōma Shōichi. "*Tsugaru ni tsuite*." Afterword to *Tsugaru* (Hirosaki: Tsugaru Shobō, 1976).